"Dr. Kutscher not only makes difficult information easier to understand, but does it with a depth of understanding and compassion that is unique in the field. His examples are true to life and his strategies concrete and applicable in everyday life. I would strongly recommend this book to be on any teacher's reading list and a guide for parents dealing with children with special challenges. If I had my wish I would make it mandatory reading for every teacher coming out of teacher's college. I will be recommending it frequently."

*—Heidi Bernhardt, Director,*
*ADRN (Attention Deficit Research Network), Toronto, Canada*

"This is a groundbreaking, terrific, thoroughly researched and brilliantly written, interpretive treatise of oft misunderstood, frequently diagnosed disorders with numerous interventions provided by a literary genius."

*—Gayle M. Bell, EdS, Educational Specialist,*
*Coeur d'Alene, ID, USA*

"While recognizing and validating the frustration that parents and teachers may experience on a daily basis when dealing with a dysregulated child, Dr. Kutscher skillfully manages to create both empathy for the child and a positive outlook for the difference informed and caring parents and teachers can make. ...I think that this book would serve as a useful quick guide for teachers as part of their school's special needs library. ...It's wonderful to have one book I can recommend to parents so that they can find helpful information on all of their child's conditions in one place."

*—Leslie Packer, PhD, specialist in Tourette's Syndrome,*
*consulting psychologist to school districts, and clinician in private practice*

*of related interest*

**Asperger's Syndrome**
**A Guide for Parents and Professionals**
*Tony Attwood*
*Foreword by Lorna Wing*
ISBN 1 85302 577 1

**Tics and Tourette Syndrome**
**A Handbook for Parents and Professionals**
*Uttom Chowdhury*
ISBN 1 84310 203 X

**The ADHD Handbook**
**A Guide for Parents and Professionals**
*Alison Munden and Jon Arcelus*
ISBN 1 85302 756 1

**Asperger Syndrome – What Teachers Need to Know**
*Matt Winter*
ISBN 1 84310 143 2

**Survival Strategies for Parenting Children with Bipolar Disorder**
*Geaorge T. Lynn*
ISBN 1 85302 921 1

**Genius!**
**Nurturing the Spirit of the Wild, Odd, and Oppositional Child – Revised Edition**
*George T. Lynn with Joanne Barrie Lynn*
ISBN 1 84310 820

**Freaks, Geeks and Asperger Syndrome**
**A User Guide to Adolescence**
*Luke Jackson*
*Foreword by Tony Attwood*
ISBN 1 84310 098 3

# Kids in the Syndrome Mix of ADHD, LD, Asperger's, Tourette's, Bipolar, and More!

The one stop guide for parents,
teachers, and other professionals

*Martin L. Kutscher* MD

*With contributions from*
*Tony Attwood* PhD *and Robert R. Wolff* MD

Jessica Kingsley Publishers
London and Philadelphia

First published in 2005
by Jessica Kingsley Publishers
116 Pentonville Road
London N1 9JB, UK
and
400 Market Street, Suite 400
Philadelphia, PA 19106, USA

*www.jkp.com*

Disclaimer: The information in this book does not constitute medical advice; nor is it a substitute for discussion between patients and their doctors. Like most areas of information, knowledge about mental health issues is likely to change over time. The views of cited references do not necessarily represent the views of the authors.

**Library of Congress Cataloging in Publication Data**
Kutscher, Martin L.
Kids in the syndrome mix of ADHD, LD, Asperger's, Tourette's, bipolar, and more! : the one stop guide for parents, teachers, and other professionals / Martin Kutscher with contributions by Tony Attwood, Robert R. Wolff.— 1st American ed.
p. cm.
Includes bibliographical references and index.
ISBN-13: 978-1-84310-810-8 (hardcover : alk. paper)
ISBN-10: 1-84310-810-0 (hardcover : alk. paper)
ISBN-13: 978-1-84310-811-5 (pbk. : alk. paper)
ISBN-10: 1-84310-811-9 (pbk. : alk. paper) 1. Behavior disorders in children. 2. Attention-deficit hyperactivity disorder. 3. Learning disabled children. 4. Tourette syndrome in children. 5. Manic-depressive illness in children. 6. Child psychopathology. 7. Asperger's syndrome. 8. Autism in children. I. Attwood, Tony. II. Wolff, Robert R. III. Title.
RJ506.B44K88 2006
618.92'89—dc22
2005009442

**British Library Cataloguing in Publication Data**
A CIP catalogue record for this book is available from the British Library

ISBN 13: 978 1 84310 810 8
ISBN 10: 1 84310 810 0

Printed and Bound in Great Britain by
Athenaeum Press, Gateshead, Tyne and Wear

Figure 3.1 (p.47) uses images from Microsoft Office 2000 ClipArt.

*To my wife, whose constant attention to our family
continues to amaze me.*

*To my children, whose very existence
is a miracle.*

*To the mothers of my patients, who give
unconditional love to their children.*

*And to my patients, who didn't choose to have the
problems that they cope with daily.*

# Contents

# Introduction

## Why this book?

There are kids out there who need help. They have attention deficit hyperactivity disorder (ADHD), or learning disabilities, or tics, or depression, or any combination of many problems. We want to assist, but how? There is a lot to learn about what we shall call the "syndrome mix."

There are superb books that cover each of these topics in detail, and I encourage you to consult the Further Reading section for suggestions. However:

- We need one book that covers multiple problems in a single place, because that's the way so many kids come: multiple issues in a single child. Co-occurrence of multiple difficulties is the norm, not the exception.

- What parent, teacher, or therapist has time to read about all those conditions from multiple books? I have had parents tell me, "If our home was calm enough for me to find time to read all of those books you suggested, then I would not have needed them in the first place." Teachers and other professionals are busy, too. (I know. I have the pleasure to be married to a high school teacher.)

- Even more problematic, these excellent books can be overwhelming in the number of suggestions to be implemented—leading all too frequently to none of them being used.

The goal of this book, then, is to provide the needed information in a format that will:

- cover multiple neuropsychiatric conditions in one text, striving to show how these syndromes frequently mix together in the same child.

- present a brief, informal distillation of crux material in a realistic but upbeat format. We explain the cause, symptoms, and treatment of each problem. A little humor along the way will help keep our perspective.

- provide a small number of high-yield recommendations. If even just these few suggestions are implemented, there will be significant effect. The book does not attempt to make the reader into full-clad special education teachers or psychiatrists.

## Who is this book for?

This book is intended for:

- parents and other relatives

- teachers

- learning specialists

- psychologists and physicians

- social workers and counselors

- speech, occupational, and physical therapists

- anyone else who comes into contact with these kids.

How can one book apply to so many groups? Well, aren't all of these people on the same team, with the shared goal of helping the same child? Don't all of these groups need to understand what is happening in the multiple spheres of the child's life at home, school, and therapy? Don't they all need to know about the underpinnings of a large variety of problems in the syndrome mix? Indeed, don't all groups need trained eyes in order to make and share appropriate observations and suggestions?

## How to use this book

Everyone initially should read the first two chapters. These cover the general principles of diagnosis and treatment that apply to virtually all conditions. Grouping these principles together at the front allows us to avoid repeating them in each chapter.

Next, you can pick out the chapters that relate to your specific, immediate needs. Hopefully, you can also read the symptom sections of all of the chapters. Unless we know something about the full range of conditions in the syndrome mix, we risk pigeonholing everyone into those diagnoses that we do know about, or we may stop looking for additional ones.

At the end of the book, there is a chapter on medication, a behavioral checklist, and further readings. Embedded in some of the chapters are links to the author's website www.PediatricNeurology.com. These links provide multimedia simulations that supplement the text.

Good luck with your kids! You are their lifeline. Failure is not an option.

## Chapter 1

# Read this Chapter! General Principles of Diagnosis

"Why am I reading a chapter on making a diagnosis?
I'm not a doctor."

## The "syndrome mix"

Start with a real, live child—a kid with feelings, needs, and hopes. Mix in a double helping of attention defict hyperactivity disorder (ADHD), a touch of Tourette's, and a dash of dysgraphia. Stir gently. That is one possible "syndrome mix" that a child, parent, teacher, and other professionals may be dealt. That's what they have to deal with.

Who says that kids have just one problem? Multiple issues often cluster together in any combination. Common members of the syndrome mix include:

- ADHD
- learning disability
- autistic spectrum disorder, such as Asperger's syndrome
- sensory integration dysfunction
- anxiety/obsessive-compulsive disorder (OCD)
- Tourette's syndrome
- depression

- bipolar depression

- oppositional defiant disorder

- central auditory processing disorder.

If a child has any one of the problems out of the syndrome mix, then there is a very significant chance of one or more of the other problems occuring.

Not only does the same child tend to be born with multiple issues, but the issues also may *exacerbate* each other. For example, a child may innately have both ADHD and learning disabilities; but then the poor attention span makes it harder to learn, while the difficulty learning makes it harder to concentrate. The mix of syndromes keeps exacerbating itself.

Similarly, the problems can *imitate* each other. For example, a child constantly mulling over her anxieties can look distracted, and this behaviour can be confused with ADHD.

In addition, often the stressed child will find himself in a stressed home or school environment. True, that stressful environment may have been caused by the youngster, but the end result is that the child now finds himself having to deal with stressed-out adults—the last ingredient the child needs!

Also, many of the neuropsychiatric conditions run in families. Thus, the child may find him/herself coping with parents (and teachers/therapists?) with their own inborn problems.

For each area of difficulty, there is a gradient of severity. We need to separate whether it is a "problem" (i.e., significantly impacts the quality of a child's life and merits significant intervention) or a "quirk" (i.e., an unusual feature causing less impairment). Even if an issue does not rise to criteria for a "problem" status, it might still benefit from being addressed. Dr. John Ratey, a noted psychiatrist, refers to these low-grade issues as "shadow syndromes" (Ratey and Johnson 1998).

One reason, then, that parents and teachers may have trouble figuring out what *the* problem is that there is typically more than one, each occurring with its own degree of intensity.

## First signs

When you think about it, psychologists, therapists, neurologists and psychiatrists do not stand on the street corner and randomly pick children to evaluate. Rather, the kids are all sent there because other people have noticed a problem. Those people are the ones on the frontline: the teachers and the parents. They may not know *what* the problem is, but these caregivers are the first to diagnose that there *is* a problem. Like it or not, the whole system depends on these first-responders. This chapter will help you feel more comfortable filling the role you have already been given.

No child's problem is diagnosed on the basis of one piece of information. Over time, multiple observers all become increasingly aware that there is some problem. The concerns typically brew over several years, until someone finally gets sufficiently frustrated to say, "Hey, there's a pattern here. Something is up!" What observations, then, typically lead to a diagnosis?

## Parents' observations

No one knows his or her child like the parents. Mothers typically have nagging (or sometimes blatant) concerns long before anyone else will listen. They are the ones who keep seeing and hearing the same things. They are the ones with whom the child confides. They typically bear the brunt of the child's frustrations.

If a parent sees that something is wrong, they are typically right. After all, most parents are not interested in "making up" problems for their children. Would a parent schedule a school meeting or a doctor's appointment just for the experience of falsely declaring to the world that their child is not thriving? No, if a parent is concerned, then there *is* usually an issue. That is not to say, though, that the parents have necessarily correctly identified *what* the problem is, or *who* is responsible to fix it—just that there is a problem.

## Teachers' observations

Teachers are incredibly valuable in the identification of a child's difficulties, for multiple reasons.

- They spend a great deal of time with the child, second only to the parents.

- They have had contact with many other children over time, helping them to establish a basis of "typical."

- They have ongoing typical "control" children in the class. They can see which child is different from all of the other kids in the same classroom.

- If a teacher is experiencing a problem with a child, then, by definition, there is a problem.

- When report card comments are read in sequence, there is usually significant conformity over the years. This pattern attests that the difficulty is with a particular child, rather than a particular teacher/student match.

In order to find the teachers' concerns, though, we must be aware that the issues are frequently masked underneath otherwise positive comments. Especially if the child is perceived as kind, cute, smart, or hard working, then the instructor tries not to be too negative. For example, he might say, "Jill can do such amazing work when she puts her mind to it!" On the surface, it's a positive comment about Jill's intelligence. The subtext, though, is that Jill is not always on task.

In addition to written comments, checklists can also be helpful. Anyone can use the Behavior Checklist (see Appendix 1). For ADHD evaluations, guidance counselors or the doctor can provide a similar quick-rating scale.

So, here are the take-home messages for teachers:

- Although the teacher's role may not be to make a specific diagnosis, their input is key to the process. Teacher feedback is the basis for diagnosing any school related problem.

- Detailed written teacher comments allow for "hidden messages" to come through, and provide the doctor with objective information. Comments may be supplemented with check-off forms.

- When a teacher identifies a problem, there usually is one. The teacher may be less accurate, though, at identifying the true underlying *cause* of the difficulty.

- Teachers might seek the guidance of their school professionals (psychologists, guidance counselors, etc.) before broaching to the parents the idea of seeking a doctor's guidance.

## Common pitfalls

If you find yourself saying any of the following, be very cautious. They are red flags of misinterpreting the child's behaviors.

- *"He's lazy."* You'll notice that "Lazy" is not listed in this or any textbook as a possible diagnosis. I've yet to meet a child who woke up one morning and had the following silent conversation: "Hmm. I wonder if I should try my best today, get good grades, and be praised? Or, maybe I should deliberately blow off my work and get punished? Oh, the latter choice should be fun!" Yes, by the time an undiagnosed teen gets to high school, the child may indeed have been beaten down so often that he has given up. However, if we look back over the person's history, we usually find a young child bouncing with energy. Somewhere along the way, he's learned to give up.

- *"He's so unprepared. He obviously does not care."* As we will see later, disorganization is a major part of ADHD and executive dysfunction.

- *"She only does it when she is interested."* All of us do better when we are interested. The question is, "What is going on that she can't do it at all unless the task is totally intriguing?"

- *"She'd be better at it if she just showed more interest."* No, it's probably the other way around, i.e., she'd be more interested in it if she were better at it. A child who is a poor reader will avoid the task. I doubt she ever said to herself, "Let's avoid reading until I get really bad at it."

- *"He is inconsistent. I've seen him do it, sometimes."* Just because a child has occasionally done something right does not mean we should hold it against him or her forever.

- *"She is just a social butterfly."* Boys tend to be labeled "hyper," whereas girls get called "social." True, it may be developmentally appropriate to be social; but is the girl really more interested in what her friend ate for breakfast than in learning her schoolwork, or is there some other problem? Inattentive ADHD (especially in girls) is harder to diagnose— but no less real—than ADHD with hyperactivity-impulsivity.

- *"I don't know if there is a problem. I'm just the teacher/parent."* As we've seen, there is no one else like the teacher and parent to identify the child who is having some problem.

## Formal evaluation
### Psycho-educational testing

If the need for potential significant intervention arises, eventually the child might be given a "psycho-educational evaluation." This consists of a detailed series of tests:

- Psychological tests (indicating a child's *potential*), such as the WISC-R (Wechsler Intelligence Scale for Children – Revised—commonly referred to as the "IQ" (intelligence quotient) test).

- Educational tests (indicating a child's *academic achievement*), such as the Woodcock-Johnson or WIAT (Wechsler Individual Achievement Test).

The report prepared by the tester usually includes an explanation of these tests and their significance. A full child study team evaluation may also include reports from social work, speech and language, occupational therapy (for fine motor, handwriting, and sensory integration), physical therapy (for gross motor), neurology, or psychiatry. Anyone—parent or teacher—can request an evaluation by the school district's team, which should be done in a timely fashion.

## The medical doctor's evaluation

So, what happens if the child gets sent to the medical doctor to be diagnosed? Nothing magical happens there that allows us to observe things not noted by parents and teachers over the years. In fact, the medical office is a poor place to observe a child's natural behavior. Let's take the case of a child presenting for an ADHD evaluation. One of the treatments for ADHD is a structured one-to-one situation with frequent, novel stimuli—just what occurs in the doctor's office. Thus, trying to make the diagnosis of ADHD is difficult while the child is in what should be a therapeutic setting. This is a point of confusion for many professionals, leading to the all too frequent, "I don't see anything wrong with your child." In addition, many problems such as poor foresight and organization need the laboratory of actual life over many months to be detected. Only caregivers outside of the doctor's office can make such long-term observations.

So what do experienced doctors do? In addition to their own observations, they rely on real-world observations by those people who care extensively for the child: the parents and the teachers. In other words, we talk to the kids; but mostly we talk to the parents, read the teacher reports, and read any testing that has been done. We try to fit all of the years of observed information into a pattern, and derive one or more diagnoses. If the medical/neurological history and physical exam suggest the need, we may sometimes perform blood tests, electroencephalograms, etc.

## Choosing appropriate accommodations

Armed with all of the data, everyone gets together for the big day: teachers, guidance counselors, school evaluators, administration, and parents. This team hopefully reaches an accord as to the appropriate diagnosis and treatments.

Each country and state has its own set of laws regarding appropriate formal accommodations, and readers are advised to discuss these procedures with their local school program director. Readers in the U.S. can find accurate information about terms such as "504" and "IDEA" at the website of the National Dissemination Center for Children with Disabilities at www.nichcy.org/resources/laws2.htm. North American readers can find local resources at www.ldonline.org.

This book, though, focuses on common sense accommodations. These accommodations are not necessarily "mandated," but can be implemented by an appropriately helpful teacher/school. Many of them would be helpful to all students, not just those with special needs. Common sense accommodations might include educating teachers about the child's diagnosis, checking that the child really understands directions, preferential seating, etc.

## Summary

The goal of helping each child to achieve his or her potential requires the cooperation and respect of the parents, teachers, and school administrators. Parents and teachers typically have quite good insight into detecting, over time, that there is *some problem*. In order to determine *which problem(s)* exist, the diagnostician depends upon the observations of those people who devote so much of their time to the children. Sorting out the syndrome mix can be difficult, since multiple problems can be born into the same child, can mimic each other, and can worsen each other.

*Chapter 2*

# Read this Chapter! General Principles of Treatment

"Why am I reading a chapter on treatment? I'm not a therapist, now, am I?"

So, a child with special needs has been entrusted to your care. If you are going to maximize the child's potential—and keep your sanity at the same time—you will need to adopt certain mindsets and strategies.

The following general guidelines apply to most kids with any of the syndromes in this book. You don't need any formal classification or diagnosis to adopt them. Specific additional guidelines for each condition are given in later chapters.

## Adjusting your own mindset

☐ *A teacher can make or break a child's year.* Don't *underestimate* your role in a child's success. I cannot tell you how many times parents and special need students tell me, "Some years were great; others were unmitigated disasters." When I ask why, the answer is overwhelmingly, "In the successful years, he felt that his teacher really understood him and was rooting for him. In the disaster years, he didn't click with the teacher, and just completely shut down."

□ ***Don't necessarily*** **overestimate** ***your role in a child's failures.*** Factors out of your control may be at play: there may be problems with academic, personal, or family stresses; or medications may not be working. Try your best, re-evaluate your strategy with parents and with the school's guidance departments; and then, just keep plugging away. Despite the best efforts of teachers, parents, and even the child, some problems cannot be totally fixed—at least not this year, anyway. Sometimes, there are just "least bad" strategies.

□ ***Remember: "The thing I like about you best... is that*** **you** ***like*** **me."** This quote from the cartoon character Ziggy applies to many human relationships, but is particularly important for kids who find themselves suddenly zapped from all angles—even from inside their own brain.

□ ***Don't take the difficult behaviors as personal affronts.*** The answer to the question "Why can't he be like all of the other children?" is that he can't. It isn't personal. You just happen to be the person in the room. Always remember that there is a real, live child underneath all of those problems.

It may also help to remember that the person who suffers most from these behaviors is usually the child himself. These children "shoot *themselves* in the foot" just as often as they bother anyone else. What further evidence could we have that these problems are not fully within their control?

□ ***Adopt a "disability outlook."*** You do not have a standard child. You can view the issue as a wonderful uniqueness in the child, or you can view the issue as a disability. Or you can view it as both. The perspective of "standard," though, is not an option.

Dr. Russell Barkley, a leading psychologist in the field of attention deficit hyperactivity disorder (ADHD), urges caregivers to incorporate a "disability outlook" (Barkley 2000). A disability outlook is not as much "fun" as just considering these kids as unique individuals with special traits. However, it points the way for caregivers to see themselves as "therapists" for their problematic child—not as victims of him.

It may be difficult to accept some of these problems as "real disabilities".

○ There is no obvious physical marker for most of the conditions.

○ Unlike the situation with obviously physical disabilities (such as blindness or cerebral palsy), the problems that result from neurobehavioral disabilities often get directed *at* the caregiver. The deaf child, for example, is having difficulties, but is not attacking us. Her problems evoke from us an instinct to aid her. In contrast, the child with a behavioral problem may not comply with, or may yell at, the person who is merely trying to help. In short, these children often don't seem to be asking for help in an easily lovable way. No wonder that these disabilities are harder to accept.

○ To accept that some people have a physiological reason for difficulty controlling their behavior runs counter to our deep convictions about who we are. Our society feels that we are under the control of our "personality," or "will," or "soul." It is hard for us to accept that these aspects of ourselves are so heavily under the influence of neurotransmitters. Just remember: *the human brain is physically a bunch of chemicals with illusions of grandeur.*

Unless we validate the problems as true disabilities, we will dismiss the problems, and instead, blame the person for not simply taking control of them. That attitude greatly burdens the special needs person. When it was applied to her, Liane Holliday Willey (an educator/writer with Asperger's syndrome) wrote, "I was made to feel that our struggles were like lint we could pick away and toss off, if only we would make the effort to do so." (Willey 1999, p.88)

□ *Minimize frustrations by taking a realistic look at the child you get every day.* Periodically, take stock of who is showing up in your life everyday. *This* is your starting point. Not a typical child. This is what you can likely expect today. Once teachers and parents accept this starting point (which I assure you the child does not exactly want, either), it is easier not to take everything so personally. Anger on the caregiver's part is reduced, since anger arises when there is discrepancy between what you expect versus what you get. We are simply dealing with the hand we've been dealt. It serves us well to think of special needs kids as "works in progress."

☐ *Overcome a fear of "coddling."* Parents and teachers are often afraid of doing harm by helping too much. How much help is appropriate? When does the role of caregiver end, and the role of the child take over? A mother of an ADHD child explained her confusion to me by way of the following analogy: "Am I supposed to harvest the food, grind it, chew it, *and* swallow it for her?"

Of course, children should be encouraged to accomplish everything that they can on their own. If they accomplish what they need to do, then we are done. If they do not, then we must step in. Unfortunately, the "sink or swim" approach often does not work with kids in the syndrome mix. If they can't do it yet, then…they can't do it yet. We wouldn't tell a child with dyslexia, "We already went over phonics yesterday. Get it right today, or get an 'F'." Similarly, negatively chastising a child with Asperger's syndrome for making the same social blunder as he made yesterday is not effective or useful. If it is a disability, it isn't going to be overcome tomorrow.

Don't worry about making their life too easy. Even with our help, these kids will still be getting more than their fair share of practice dealing with failures, frustration, criticism, and pain. We should only wish that our interventions for special needs kids could be so successful that their life will now be easier than everyone else's.

☐ *Provide a safety net.* Let's try a few analogies. When acrobats are taught a new trapeze act, their trainers provide them with a safety net. When gymnasts perform their high bar routines, they have a "spotter." No one worries that providing these safeguards will interfere with learning, or will make the performer take his task less seriously. It is simply that, without a safety net, the penalty for missing a handgrip while flying across the trapeze bars is neither commensurate with the mistake nor productive. Similarly, we may need to intervene in the child's college application process, because the penalty of messing up his future career is not commensurate with the "sin" of poor organization.

Be the safety net or "spotter" for the special needs kid. If she gets it right, she won't need you, and there's no harm done that you were standing by. If she doesn't get it right, you are there to provide a softer landing—and make sure that the consequence is appropriate to the mistake.

☐ *Communication between teacher and parent is key.* In order to provide the appropriate safety net, teachers and parents will need to communicate. Use phone calls, e-mail, postcards, or anything...but stay in touch! Waiting for mid-term progress reports is too late for the parents to help the child dig out of the problem.

Don't expect the special needs child to be a reliable purveyor of information!

☐ *If it is working, keep doing it. If not, do something else.* This is hard work, but you will make it through this; you have no choice. Failure is not an option. However, don't expect that all problems can be fixed overnight. Many of these kids will be working on their issues as part of a "Fifty Year Plan."

☐ *Forgive yourself.* Dr. Barkley urges his readers to forgive themselves nightly for their inability to be perfect (Barkley 2000, p.153). Each night, review how you've done that day and how you could do better. Then, remember that each of us is only human, and forgive yourself for the past. This applies to parents, children, and teachers.

☐ *Review this text, and others, periodically.* You are going to forget this stuff, and different principles will likely be needed at different stages.

## Understanding the child's mindset

☐ *Learn about the child's problems.* As you learn about the child's areas of difficulty, you will feel more confident in your teaching/parenting methods—and feel less threatened. Also, you will likely find that many of the difficult behaviors are actually part of the child's underlying diagnosis. For example, you might have "blamed" a child with Asperger's for taking on the role of "class policeman," until you discover that this black-and-white rigidity is a typical part of the syndrome.

This text is a great place to start learning. Further reading suggestions are given at the end of the book. The school special education staff should also have recommended materials for classroom teachers and parents.

☐ *Seek to understand.* Ask yourself, "Why did he do that?" There is *always* a reason, even if that reason is neither rational nor productive in the long term. For example, Johnnie may act up whenever the math becomes difficult. In the long run, that is a bad strategy; but in the short run, being sent to the principal solves the immediate discomfort of feeling inadequate. Often, the behaviors make sense if we remember that these children are so overwhelmed by what is happening that they live almost exclusively in the present, without much ability for foresight.

☐ *Not all brains see everything the same.* A special needs child may not experience the world exactly as we do. Their abilities and coping skills may not be even across the board. Much of the behavior will strike us as odd, or different, or even inexplicable. You're right. That's why the kids have a diagnosable condition.

What *is* the child's brain seeing? Although by no means always accurate, we can open a window into a child's mind simply by carefully paying attention to—and legitimizing—their reaction. Unfortunately, we often incorrectly dismiss their reaction as irrelevant by labeling it "over-reacting."

People do not "over-react." Instead, they "over-feel." When a child blows up over what seems like a trivial issue to us, it may help us to understand that in *this* child's mind, this issue must have a tremendous amount of meaning. He's not acting. We could benefit from saying, "Wow, if that's how it feels to him, we should calmly discuss this!"

So, first we must seek to understand; then we plan a reaction.

☐ *We see only part of what is going on in a child's life.* By the time a kid with issues shows up in class, who knows what has gone on already that morning or the previous evening at home? Waking up and getting dressed may have been major fights. Homework may have been hours of frustration for everyone. And when the child comes home, the parent needs to remember that their special child may have had an especially difficult time at school.

☐ *Finally, remember that some of the difficult child / adolescent behavior is simply normal.* We may be quick to pin all difficult moments with the child as being due to some "disorder." Keep in mind, though, that life with any child is never totally smooth. Every family up and down the street, and every teacher up and down the hallway, is having some problems as well. That may be comforting; it's nice to know that you are not alone.

In particular, even typical pre-teens and teens go through a period where their respect for adult authority is less than maximal. Anecdotal experience suggests that, from the typical child's perspective:

- when the child is less than 10 years old, mom/teacher seems to know *everything*

- when the child turns around ten years old, mom suddenly seems to know *less than nothing*

- when the child returns from college, mom seems to have learned *a fair amount* as well, and seems to be a pretty good source of advice.

## How to change the child's behavior

There are two major rules to affecting a child's behavior:

1. Keep it positive.

2. Keep it calm.

It sounds simple enough!

## Rule 1: Keep it positive

☐ *Enjoy the child.* Seek to enjoy, not to be frustrated. Celebrate the child's humor, creativity, passion, and even his/her unique qualities. Given all of the child's problems, it is sometimes hard to find anything to praise. Find some accomplishment to laud, and some activity to enjoy together. You know, "Catch them being good." Laugh with each other. Let the youngster be helpful and "useful." Let the child know that you believe in him/her, despite the difficulties.

In her autobiography, Liane Holliday Willey explains: "The people who have proven that they will stand by me no matter what I say, think or do, have given me a finer gift than they will ever realize." (Willey 1999, p.58)

☐ *Use positive reinforcement when possible.* Instead of negatively reinforcing wrong behavior, Dr. Barkley reminds us to set a reward for the correct behavior you would rather replace it with (Barkley 2000, p.148). For example, suppose that you are trying to correct a child's nasty behavior towards his sister. Your goal is that he should be nice to her. So, rather than punishing a child for yelling at his sister, reward him for each kind comment. Rewards should be immediate, frequent, powerful, clearly defined, and consistent.

Younger children may respond to sticker charts or token systems, which may be considered part of Dr. Ross Greene's "Plan A" for behavior modification using rewards and punishments (Greene 1999). Greene's criteria for adopting behavior modification/reward systems are summarized below.

- The behavior must be worth the effort of changing.

- The child must have the ability to consistently control the behavior.

- The reward/punishment is likely to work (e.g., punishment is unlikely to correct forgetful behavior).

- Those with allegedly cooler heads can apply the plan consistently.

- It is the child's problem.

When using reward/token systems, remember the following:

o Children with special needs require frequent, strong, and immediate feedback and rewards.

o The rules need to be succinctly reviewed at the scene before they are needed.

o Most people are drawn towards the most attractive stimulus. Reward systems capitalize on this trait by using a "carrot" to lead the child in a productive direction.

o "But don't 'bribes' lead them to do things for the wrong reasons?" Yes, but they already haven't responded to the "right" reasons. That appeal has already failed by the time enticements are added.

o The rewards will need frequent rotation to maintain their power.

o Enticements can be as simple as "First we work, then we get to play." Or, "If you only tease your sister twice this week, then you get your allowance."

Formal systems are described in many books, including those by Dr. Larry Silver and Dr. Russell Barkley, who have given many of the recommendations above (see Further Reading, pp.210–11). Token systems entail earning points for good behavior (or losing them for bad behavior) that are then traded in for any privilege. Practically speaking, formal token systems are difficult to maintain, and work best with elementary school children. The school psychologist can help with specifics.

☐ *Negative reinforcement does not improve attitude.* Threats may change behavior, but they do not motivate towards a good attitude. Only rewards (internal or external) lead to an improved mood.

☐ *Avoid the "resentment treadmill."* Resentment breeds resentment. Perhaps, the following sounds familiar:

John is nasty to his mom. Mom stays quiet. John is nasty again. This time, Mom yells back. The next morning, Mom is still angry. She walks into the John's bedroom and starts in, "Why can't you even set your own alarm clock? After how you treated me yesterday, you still want me to wake you up?" John is bewildered. He curses at his mother. John goes to school, acts disrespectfully (again); and gets in trouble with the teacher, who is still sensitized from yesterday's unpleasant classroom interaction.

Good morning! It's another day on the resentment treadmill.

By the time someone is reading this chapter, the resentment treadmill may have been running at high speed for some time. Each "side" (child or caregivers) can recite a litany of truly legitimate complaints against the other. The cycle leads nowhere good. Everyone can agree to that. Someone has to get off the treadmill first. It isn't going to be the dysfunctional child. That leaves the mature adult to take the first leap. That's you. Don't expect instant results or gratitude.

Below are some strategies to help resist the appeal of jumping back on the treadmill. It's all easier said than done: resentment and anger can be addictive.

- *Don't be a nasty cop.* Imagine being pulled over by a policeman for making an illegal turn. The policeman approaches your window, hands you the ticket, and proceeds to insult you. "Don't you have any respect for the safety of yourself or others? Don't you care about anything? You are such a jerk! And, your car looks really disgusting! Why don't you clean it up?" What would you think about the policeman? Would you want to have dinner with him tonight? Would you want to give him a hug at bedtime? Would you look forward to seeing him in school tomorrow? Moral of the story: As you hand out the punishment, skip the nasty attitude. The punishment is bad enough. The nasty attitude just breeds resentment.

- *Avoid Dr. Phelan's four cardinal sins* (Phelan 1994, p.39):
  - Don't nag. It hasn't worked yet. If you don't have anything nice to say, don't say it. Even simple comments like "How was your day?" may cause frustration in your child.
  - Don't lecture. It doesn't work either. Plus, given their sense of time, ADHDers will find the experience interminable. Instead, give one or two brief, clear instructions. "Insight

transplants" from you to your child, as Phelan calls them, are unlikely to work.

– Don't argue. It takes two to fight. No argument can take place without your consent.

– Don't offer unscheduled, spontaneous "advice." What are the odds that your Nintendo playing teen will respond pleasantly to your request to discuss right now that school project due next month?

Phelan calls these four points "The Four Cardinal Sins." These "sins" are ineffective and actually harmful. Why would we use them? Instead, either decide that the issue is aggravating but not significant enough to warrant intervention (i.e., stay quiet); or make an appointment with your child to discuss the issue.

○ *Minimize arguments with the "no-fault" approach.* Chris Zeigler Dendy has the very useful suggestion that rules be enforced with a no-fault approach (Zeigler Dendy 1995). In other words, avoid arguments based on whose fault it is. Just deal with the end results. Consider this scene where a teen has a 10pm curfew. He arrives home at 10:45pm.

> Teen: "I'm sorry, mom. I was getting a ride home from Jack, and he had to stop for gas. Jill had a stomachache and we had to drop her off at her house. Then, Jack remembered that he had to stop for milk for his baby brother. I couldn't call because my cell phone battery died. So, I'm sorry that I'm late."

How do you argue with that set of excuses? You can't. Instead, proceed as follows:

> Mom: "I'm sorry, too. I'm sorry that you had bad luck. I'm sorry that you are stuck with the punishment we've agreed on if you come home past your curfew. I'm not blaming you, but those are the rules."

It doesn't matter why a child arrives late. He is late, this is the consequence, and we'll try to create a plan to prevent it from happening again. It eliminates negative discussion, doesn't it?

This approach is particularly useful when dealing with people who blame others for their problems. There is no point in *their* blaming *you* if blame is not being made relevant. Could this sometimes be unfair? Sometimes, yes. But in the long run, arguments are diminished, and that is to everyone's advantage.

Also, this approach prevents direct criticism of the child. We punish the end behavior and its end results. We are not directly criticizing the child. After all, we are not assigning blame to anyone. Thus, this approach is a rediscovery of the old adage, "Criticize the behavior, not the child." It is another way to keep things positive.

○ *Keep your relational bank account in the positive.* It may help to consider that you have a bank account of experiences with the child: there are good times and bad times that can be deposited into your relationship. Your goal is to have the overall balance be in the positive. Make sure that you take the good times with the bad. When she is finally ready to apologize, talk, or cuddle, take her up on her offer right then and there. Your goal is to put some good times into your relationship. Take them as they come. Otherwise, you end up only with the bad.

As you enter into each interaction, ask yourself, "Will my next comment/action make my bank account with the child run into debt or into a positive flow? Am I about to jump back on the resentment treadmill?"

○ *Provide help for deficits at the moment it is needed.* Children with special difficulties need enabling at the time of need, not negative feedback when it is already too late. Unfortunately, the simple reality is that negative consequences do not usually teach the needed behaviors to kids with disabilities. Typically, they *know* what to do; they just cannot carry out the plan. They already know, for example, that they should come to class prepared. They already know that if they do not do their homework, they will not get into the good college that they want. However, for them, it just does not happen. Punishing such a child would make as much sense as punishing a child with dyslexia for not remembering the difference between a "b" and a "d." (Note that in the U.S., federal law prohibits a school from punishing a child for symptoms of a disability.)

Once we understand that negative reinforcement has not been working, we are ready to provide relief for their disabilities by guiding them at the moment guidance is needed—rather than continued disbelief that they did it wrong again. We may be amazed at how many times the kids keep using the same unsuccessful strategies, but how many times is it going to take for *us* to figure out that *we* keep using unsuccessful strategies with them?

o ***Punishment is not your chance to inflict misery; it is your chance to improve your child's upcoming decisions.*** What is the purpose of punishment? Unless you are a sadist, you are not really trying to "get even" or to make little kids miserable. Rather, the purpose of a punishment presumably is to correct future behaviors. A modest, immediate punishment is likely to be at least as effective as a prolonged one. A spiral of increasing punishments is unlikely to work, and just saddles everyone with a lengthy period of unhappiness in the future. Consider the following scenario:

> Father: "If you don't apologize right now, there will be no T.V. tonight."
>
> Child gives no response.
>
> Father: "Okay. If you don't apologize in the next 10 seconds, there will be no T.V. this entire week."
>
> Child gives no response. Soon, the punishment is up to no T.V. for a month. There is still no apology, the child has a meltdown, and everybody is angry.
>
> Twenty-nine days of no T.V. pass. The family has been miserable.
>
> Child: "Dad, do you remember what I'm being punished for?"
>
> Father: "Johnny, I don't have a clue."

The punishment has far exceeded its usefulness, don't you think? Remember, when punishment is required, keep it immediate and controlled.

Sometimes, keeping it positive does not work. As the situation progresses, we will need to invoke Rule 2: Keep it calm.

## Rule 2: Keep it calm

*Be a defusing influence, not an inflammatory one.* The life of a special needs child is overwhelming. The treatment for his over-reaction is to defuse the situation, not inflame it. This applies whether the child has ADHD, oppositional defiant disorder, bipolar depression, anxiety disorder, or just about any condition. Actually, this principle applies to just about any human interaction.

Seek to defuse, not to inflame. When tempers or anxieties flare, allow everyone to cool off. Remember, the caregiver may have to cool off as well. Serious discussion can only occur during times of composure. Remember: negative behaviors usually occur because the child is spinning out of control, not because he is evil. For kids that Dr. Ross Greene (1999) refers to as "explosive", the first step is to "Just STOP!".

Most typical children will respond well to typical enticements and threats of punishment. If you made it this far, your child probably isn't one of them. Here, our focus is on *preventing* over-heated meltdowns. We anticipate problems and try to head them off: we stop, we stay calm, and we negotiate if possible.

Here are details of the defusing technique—labeled "Plan B" by Dr. Ross Greene (1999).

□ *Head off big fights* **before** *they begin.* When things start going badly, redirect to a positive direction rather than criticizing the misbehavior. For example, if the child is arguing with a peer, then suggest a new activity such as having a snack, rather than handing out a punishment.

□ *Pick your fights.* Is this fight worth chipping away at your relationship with the child? Remember, this is not war. Psychologist Dr. Steven Covey (1989) reminds parents to keep in mind what you want your child to think about you when he delivers your eulogy. If you are a teacher, keep in mind how you want the child to remember the school year.

☐ *Give transition warnings.* Many special kids have trouble with transitions. Discuss in advance what is expected. Give plenty of warnings. Have the child repeat out loud the terms he just agreed to. Some children need to negotiate for those "two more minutes." A little extra patience on the caregiver's part may help avoid a useless meltdown.

☐ *Watch the "stress speedometer."* Imagine that a child (or you) is a car with a stress speedometer. When that speedometer reaches 60 miles per hour (mph), the back wheels will spin out and nothing can prevent a crash. Attempts to intervene during the spin out will just prolong the system failure. The goal, then, is to keep anyone from hitting 60 mph. So imagine you enter the scene when the child is at a stress level of 40 mph. For the child, the anxiety of the current situation is getting to him. You laugh—or you divert, or you negotiate—and the stressometer comes down to 30 mph. Great! You are on the right track. Keep it up. However, the next day, the same intervention brings the child up to 50 mph. Back off! You are just a moment away from 60 mph, and the horrible meltdown that will then be unstoppable. Just STOP, and walk away.

  This is not the time to give in to our impulse to just get done with it. You might have the self-control to do that, but your special child may not have been born that way. Don't assume that just because you can handle it, he can as well. All brains have equal rights, but all brains are not constructed the same.

☐ *"Just STOP!" is the key—for the overwhelmed person* **and** *for you.* Incredible things happen if everyone is able to just STOP:

  o It works! Even five or ten minutes are all most people require to regain their composure and ability to think clearly. These few minutes spent to avoid a crisis certainly beat enduring a much more negative and lengthier meltdown.

  o With the benefit of time, most people will come around to the right conclusion on their own, and comply.

  o Once you have calmed down, the correct method of behavioral management will seem almost blatantly obvious. For example, we try to keep it positive. We discuss seeking to understand

and making the child part of the problem-solving process. We discuss choosing only productive punishments. When you are calm, these approaches are not exactly rocket science, and are almost self-evident. When you are overwhelmed yourself, these approaches are not available.

Further stressing the child does not work and is actually counterproductive. She is already overwhelmed. She is already overloaded and over-stimulated. Being further stressed just inflames the situation, and ultimately makes it harder for your child to achieve her goal: regaining composure so that her own brain can reach the right decision.

"But what if he doesn't just stop?" Encourage compliance with the system by explaining in advance that this cooling off period is not punishment. It is not like the old punitive "time out" system, which works best with preschool and elementary students. Rather, the child gets to go do some pleasant—yet soothing—activity. You may need your own soothing activity, too. In any case, remember that it takes two people to engage. Walk away.

After stopping, state the rule once and leave. The decision to declare a cooling-off period has nothing to do with a decision as to who "won." You are not giving in. Calmly state the rule or action that is to be followed, and end the discussion. Come back later when cool heads prevail.

□ *Stay calm.* That bears repeating. Stay calm. Once calm, you then need to negotiate with certain children—negotiate, negotiate, negotiate. Caregivers need to model negotiation, not inflexibility. What is wrong with teaching a child to seek win-win solutions? Don't worry about losing control: the adult always gets to decide which compromise is accepted.

In class, this would best be done in private. The teacher always gets to decide when the discussion is over, or when the child needs to be sent to administration.

### USING PLAN B IN THE CLASSROOM

Hopefully, these techniques will not be required too often in class. We are only talking about the rare classroom situation where there is simply not much of an alternative. Certainly, it is difficult to let one student appear to "get away with it" in front of other students. However, having the students witness an unproductive meltdown does not model a useful interaction either. If the event is already "public," the adult should make it clear to everyone witnessing the situation that no one is "getting away" with anything. There will be discussion and consequences meted out, even though the discussion will take place later in private. We are modeling peaceful, useful human interactions.

## Quick quiz on angry behavior

This good-natured open book quiz is designed to test and reinforce your understanding of angry behavior. The questions relate to the following *true* story:

> *A 13-year-old boy with ADHD discovers that his orthodontic bite-plate is missing from its handy container. He angrily accuses everyone else of having taken it. His mother explains the blatantly obvious fact that no one else would be interested in his used dental appliance. He continues screaming and blaming her for its absence.*

1.  The accusatory behavior of this otherwise bright child can best be explained by:

    (a) He's not quite smart enough to comprehend that his bite-plate isn't worth stealing.

    (b) He's overwhelmed by frustration.

2.  Yelling back and accusing your child of behaving horribly would:

    (a) Cause him to say, "Thanks for helping me see the error of my ways."

    (b) Cause him to be even more overwhelmed.

3. You try unsuccessfully to help find the bite-plate. A *useful* parental response at this point would be:

    (a) Engage in an escalating screaming match.

    (b) STOP! Walk away. Retain your composure. Resist the urge to get in the last word. Resume discussion when everyone is calm.

4. This type of outrageous, explosive behavior in ADHD is the result of:

    (a) A nasty, selfish child.

    (b) A common reaction of overwhelmed children.

5. Your goal as caregiver is to:

    (a) Further inflame the child's frustration, leading to a spiraling downhill relationship.

    (b) See yourself as a therapist, teaching the child to STOP and defuse the situation.

6. In the heat of real life, you would have acted the correct way.

    (a) Usually true.

    (b) Usually false.

**Answers: (b) to all questions.**

## Chapter 3

# Attention Deficit Hyperactivity Disorder

"Okay, Bobby has ADHD [attention deficit hyperactivity disorder]. That explains why he doesn't seem to pay attention and is so fidgety. But I still don't understand so many things about him. Why is he so disorganized? Why won't he write down his homework assignments? Why doesn't punishing him seem to have any effect? Why doesn't he see the consequence of his actions? Why does his mother say that homework is such a fight? Is it true that he blows up so easily at home?"

Bobby's mom has ADHD, also. Once, while joking about her chaotic life, she said, "I aspire to have obsessive compulsive disorder—so that I might be more organized." She was serious.

## Defining ADHD
### "Official" (and woefully incomplete) definition of ADHD

The American Psychiatric Association gives "official" criteria for many syndromes in its book, *Diagnostic and Statistical Manual of Mental Disorders, 4th edition,* (APA 1994) commonly referred to as DSM-IV. As typically defined by DSM-IV, ADHD consists of a triad of inattention and/or hyperactivity-impulsivity.

## Symptoms of the "inattentive" type

□ *Attention and distractibility* problems are a core symptom of ADHD. There is an inability to inhibit distractions in order to stay focused on the task at hand. The person does not seem to listen or pay close attention. There may be frequent careless mistakes.

□ *Organizational difficulties are an equal part of the problem*. This includes difficulty organizing, sustaining, or completing tasks. The person may be forgetful, "absent minded," or easily lose things.

## Symptoms of the hyperactive-impulsive type

□ *Hyperactivity difficulties* include being fidgety or talking excessively. The child may run, climb, seem "on the go," or be out of the seat excessively. Additionally, he may have difficulty playing quietly.

□ *Impulsivity difficulties* include blurting out answers, difficulty waiting turn, intruding, or interrupting.

In addition, symptoms should begin before the child is seven years old, interfere with overall life functioning, and occur in at least two settings (such as home, school, sports, etc.)

Using these criteria, DSM-IV defines three subtypes of ADHD, which are:

- predominantly inattentive type

- predominantly hyperactive-impulsive type (rare form)

- combined type (most common form).

By current terminology, even if the person does not have hyperactivity, the diagnosis will still be "ADHD". The term "ADD" is no longer an official DSM-IV term.

Note that *disorganization* is actually built into the definition of ADHD. In fact, it is fair to say that you really can't be ADHD unless you have to work especially hard at being organized. (An exception to this rule may occur when an anxiety disorder about the future compensates for the ADHD.)

# A more useful definition of ADHD

## A PROBLEM WITH INHIBITION

Children with ADHD typically can pay attention to their video games forever. As long as they are allowed to stay at the most fascinating activity, they are fine. The problem, though, occurs when they are supposed to pay attention to something that is less captivating (e.g., multiplication), while simultaneously filtering out something that is more intriguing (e.g., the birds out the window). That requires putting brakes on the "distractions."

Observations such as this have led Dr. Russell Barkley and others to define ADHD as a deficiency of *inhibition*, not a deficiency of attention span, per se (Barkley 1998, 2000). Kids (and adults) with ADHD, then, are relatively brakeless. They are:

- unable to put brakes on distractions ➔ inattentive
- unable to put brakes on inside thoughts ➔ impulsive
- unable to put brakes on *acting* upon distractions or thoughts ➔ hyperactive.

These brakes reside in our brain's frontal and prefrontal lobes—the part of our brain just behind our forehead. These inhibitory centers keep us from being flooded by sensory information. They also allow us the luxury of time during which we can consider our options before reacting. Unlike most other complex organisms, humans have the option of modulating their responses. In ADHD, though, the frontal and prefrontal lobes are essentially under-functioning. The inhibitory centers are asleep on the job.

Thus, the concept of ADHD as poor inhibition explains the classic symptoms of ADHD above, but also leads us to understanding the serious problems with "executive function" typically seen in ADHD.

## PROBLEMS WITH "EXECUTIVE FUNCTION"

What are "executive functions"? Our brain's frontal and prefrontal lobes function largely as our Chief Executive Officer. These frontal centers consider where we came from, figure out where we want to go, and plan how to control ourselves in order to get there. In short, executive functions are the skills require to make a plan and actually execute it. The old name for executive function was "wisdom." According to Barkley (2000), executive functions include the following:

- ☐ **The ability to inhibit**—problems with which lead to the classic symptoms of ADHD, and also result in the inability to inhibit behavior long enough for the other executive functions below to adequately develop.

- ☐ **Working memory**—the myriad of things that our brain can juggle at any given moment. We need to juggle what is happening now, our future goal, past unsuccessful strategies, etc. It is analogous to the 512 megabytes of RAM (random access memory) on our computers (versus "long-term memory," which corresponds to our computer's much larger 80 gigabyte hard drive).

- ☐ **Foresight**—perhaps the most essential executive function. It refers to the ability to predict one's future needs, and to predict the consequences of one's actions. Lack of foresight is a key part of ADHD problems. There is no such thing as "the past" or "the future." There is only right now. In fact, Barkley's full definition of ADHD is the inability to inhibit the present with an eye to the future. It's not that ADHDers do not care about the future. It's that, right now, the future does not exist.

- ☐ **Hindsight**—our ability to keep the success rates of previous strategies in our working memory. Without hindsight, we are doomed to keep making the same mistakes.

- ☐ **Organization (planning)**—problems are virtually guaranteed in ADHD. In fact, looking at the diagnostic criteria, it is virtually impossible to be ADHD without an element of disorganization. It starts to become more evident in late elementary school, and even more so in middle school. In middle school, the child's single elementary teacher (a.k.a. surrogate mother from 8am to 3pm) gets replaced by a team of teachers. Just at this time of need for increased amounts of organizational support, most schools pull back—adopting the "he needs to sink or swim on his own" attitude. (Unfortunately, kids with the disability we call ADHD will usually keep sinking without organizational support.)

☐ *Self-talk*—the ability to talk to ourselves. It is a mechanism by which we work through our choices using words. Toddlers can be heard using self-talk out loud. Eventually, this ability becomes internalized and automatic. However, ADHDers have not inhibited their reactions long enough for this skill to fully develop. Frequently, they are not making conscious logical choices—they are just reacting.

☐ *Sense of time*—extremely poor in ADHD. Time can drag on f-o-r-e-v-e-r, or it can go by too quickly. Not all of us experience time in the same fashion.

☐ *Shifting from Agenda A to Agenda B*—a difficult task requiring good executive function. Pulling yourself out of one activity and switching to another—transitioning—is innately difficult, and requires effort and control.

☐ *Separating emotion from fact*—every fact or event has an *objective* significance, and also a *subjective emotional* significance that our brain tags it with. For example, a traffic jam has an objective reality of a 20-minute time delay. Different minds, though, give, different emotional tags to the event. Some see the traffic jam as a nice way to relax a little more, whereas others see it as one more intentional act of cruelty imposed personally upon them by the universe. Without the gift of time, we never get to separate emotion from fact. This leads to poor ability to judge the significance of what is happening to us.

## Real-life symptoms of ADHD and executive dysfunction

We have just given the definitions of executive functions, but let's see how they play out in real life. As we show here, these problems with executive function are not just "incidental" symptoms. They are hard to live with—ask the teacher, parent, or child—and they are all commonly seen as part of the condition we summarize "ADHD."

☐ *Lack of foresight!!!*—"Bobby, you'll never get into a good college if you all you do is stare out the window. Can't you see that you better start working on your term paper already? And why didn't you tell me that you need report covers for tomorrow? You act like your own worst enemy!" Foresight is a major adaptive ability of humans. Lack of use of this ability can be the most devastating part of ADHD. Teachers and mothers—often endowed with great foresight—are crushed as they watch the child repeatedly head down counterproductive paths. ADHD children are usually extremely poor at anticipating their needs!

☐ *Burn bridges* **in front** *of them!*—"Bobby, you yell at me all day and now you expect me to drive you to karate?" Lots of typical people burn their bridges behind them. That's not a good idea, but it is unfortunately common. It takes executive dysfunction, though, to burn your bridges before you even realize that you are going to need them.

☐ *Poor hindsight / trouble learning from mistakes*—"Bobby, how many times do you have to be punished for the same thing? No matter how many times I give you a '0,' it doesn't ever seem to change your behavior." Unable to inhibit the present, Bobby cannot stop to consider lessons from the past.

☐ *Live at the "mercy of the moment"*—"Bobby is always swept away by whatever is happening to him right then and there. He's like a moth—smack up against the brightest light." ADHD behaviors make sense once we realize that they are based on reactions taking only the present moment into account. It is not that Bobby doesn't *care* about the future; it is that the future and the past don't even exist. Such is the nature of the disability.

If you want to understand the ADHDer's actions, simply ask yourself: "What behavior makes sense if you feel like you only have four seconds left to live?" By way of analogy, imagine happily fishing as you ride down a river. You would be so involved that you would not see the upcoming cliff. It's not that you don't "care" about falling over a cliff—it's that you don't even get to consider it. The future does not show up on their radar screen. Take the example in Figure 3.1.

This is what Jack sees:

This is what everyone else seems to notice:

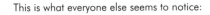

*Figure 3.1: Jack is in a boat, happily fishing. Reeling in the fish captures all of his attention.*

☐ **Poor organization**—"Bobby, don't you remember that there is a paper due tomorrow!" And, "Why don't you come to me after class so that I can sign your assignment book?" And, "Why didn't you hand in your homework, even though you mother called me to say that you really did do it? Don't you care?"

☐ **Poor sense of time**—"Bobby, what have you been doing all afternoon? You can't spend two hours on the first assignment! You'll never make it to baseball practice!"

☐ **Time moves too slowly**—"This lecture is going on forever!"

☐ **Poor ability to utilize "self-talk" to work through a problem**—"Bobby, what were you thinking?! Did you ever think this through?"

☐ **Poor sense of self-awareness**—Bobby's true answer to the above question is probably "I don't have a clue. I guess I wasn't actually thinking."

☐ *Poor reading of social clues*—"Bobby, you're such a social klutz. Can't you see that the other children think that's weird?"

☐ *Poor internalization and generalization of rules*—"Bobby, why do I need to keep reminding you that reading time comes *after* you finish your homework? And you'd think that, when I told you to clean out your desk, you would have known to clean out your cubby as well."

☐ *Inconsistent work and behavior*—"Bobby, if you could do it well yesterday, why is today so horrible?" With 100% of their energy, they may be able to control the task that most of us can do with 50% of our focus. But who can continually muster 100% effort? As the joke goes: ADHD children do something right twice, and we hold it against them for the rest of their lives.

☐ *Trouble with transitions*—"Bobby, why do you curse at me when I'm just calling you for dinner?"

☐ *Hyper-focused at times*—"When Bobby is on the computer, I can't get him off."

☐ *Poor frustration tolerance*—"Bobby, why can't you even let me help you get over this?"

☐ *Frequently overwhelmed*—"Please, just stop! I can't stand it. Just stop. Please!" In order to really feel what it must be like to be flooded by everything all at once, listen to the soundtrack that simulates the experience of ADHD at www.PediatricNeurology.com/sound.htm. Then take the related survey with your child. It is a mind-altering experience that you cannot just read about.

Some real-life symptoms become more prominent in the older child (and at home).

☐ *Gets angry frequently and quickly*—"Bobby, why do you get so upset with your friends? Does it really have to be just your way?"

☐ *Pushes away those whose help they need the most*—"Mommy, stop checking my assignment pad. Get out!"

□ *"Hyper-responsiveness"*—"Mommy, you know I hate sprinkles on my donuts! You never do anything for me! I hate you!" Barkley (2000) uses the term hyper-responsiveness to indicate that people with ADHD have excessive emotions. Their responses, however, are appropriate to what they are actually feeling. So next time you see someone "over-reacting," realize that they are actually "over-feeling," and must feel really awful at that moment.

□ *Inflexible/explosive reactions*—"Bobby, you're stuck on this. No, I can't just leave you alone. Bobby, now you're incoherent. Bobby, just stay away. I can't stand it when you break things!" Greene (1999) gives an extensive explanation about the inflexible/explosive child.

□ *Feels calm only when in motion*—"He always seems happiest when he is busy. Is that why he stays at work so late?"

□ *Thrill-seeking behavior*—"He seems to crave stimulation at any cost. In fact, he feels most 'on top of his game' during an emergency."

□ *Trouble paying attention to others*—"My husband never listens when I talk to him. He just cannot tolerate sitting around with me and the kids. He doesn't 'pay attention' to his family any more than he 'paid attention' in school." As the patient gets older, people in his life will increasingly expect more time and empathy to be directed their way. Yet, the above behaviors may interfere with the ADHDer's demonstration of these traits, despite their passions.

□ *Trouble with mutual exchange of favors with friends*—without establishing a reliable "bank account" of kept promises, friendships can be hard to make.

□ *Sense of failure to achieve goals*—"Somehow, I never accomplished all that I thought I could or should have." This deep disappointment is commonly what prompts adults with ADHD to seek help.

□ *Lying, cursing, stealing, and blaming others*—can become frequent components of ADHD; especially as the child gets older. Some particularly depressing data show how ADHD children compare with typical children. According to Barkley *et al.* (1990), 72% of kids with ADHD argue with adults (vs. 21% of typical children); 66% of kids with ADHD blame others for their own mistakes (vs. 17% of typical children); 71% of kids with ADHD act touchy or are easily annoyed (vs. 20% of typical children); 40% of kids with ADHD swear (vs. 6% of typical children); 49% of kids with ADHD lie (vs. 5% of typical children) and 50% of kids with ADHD steal (vs. 7% of typical children).

In short, the symptoms of ADHD become less "cute" as the children switch from elementary to secondary schools. The "good" news comes from understanding that these problems are commonly part of the syndrome we call ADHD. They are nobody's fault—not yours, and not your child's. This understanding points the way towards coping with these issues.

As if the above isn't enough, ADHD can be associated with any of the other conditions of the syndrome mix found in this book. Particularly commonly associated learning problems include the following:

☐ **Problems following a sequence of directions.** Consider the following typical directive from a teacher: "Okay, class. Be quiet, go to your seat, open your math book, turn to page 41, and do the first problem on the top of the page." The next thing you know, this kid is doing poorly in math because he is having trouble following a sequence of commands.

☐ **Poor handwriting.** Interestingly, this often improves with medication.

## Neurological basis of ADHD

No matter what country we look at, ADHD by DSM-IV criteria occurs in 1 in 16 people (about 6%) (Barkley 1998, p.82). When one person in the home has ADHD, the whole family feels its effects. Assuming four people per family, that means that in any given home, there is a 4 in 16 risk that the household will be affected by someone with ADHD. That is how it works out: a condition that affects 6% of the population means that if four mothers get together, the odds are that one of their lives will be affected by ADHD in their family. That is a lot of families. Although 6% of the population has ADHD, only about 3% of the U.S. school-age population is taking stimulant medication for the condition (Olfson 2003).

As we have seen, ADHD results from insufficient functioning of the frontal and prefrontal lobes. It appears that the frontal lobes have not been fully woken up by the neurotransmitter norepinephrine. In turn, the frontal lobes do not transmit enough of the chemical dopamine to adequately inhibit other brain activity.

It is well established that ADHD stems from a neurological basis. Adoption and other studies show a strong genetic component. One possible suspect is a gene for the D4 dopamine receptor. PET (positron emission tomography) scans and functional MRI (magnetic resonance imaging) scans show prefrontal abnormalities and disturbed dopamine activity. Although these studies are not helpful in diagnosing an individual child, they should help us to be more understanding of the ADHDer's innate problems.

Sometimes, children will be noted to "space out." Is it a seizure disorder, or is it ADHD? Observation of the features in Table 3.1 should help the physician sort out the two conditions. Sometimes, the distinction can be difficult, even with the aid of an electroencephalogram.

Table 3.1 Distinguishing ADHD from seizures

| Staring off in seizures | Staring off in ADHD |
| --- | --- |
| Occurs any time, including in the middle of an activity, such as while talking or eating. | Occurs only during "down time," such as while watching T.V. or when bored. |
| Touching or loudly calling to the child does NOT end the spell. | The spell stops when the child is called loudly or touched. |
| There may be associated symptoms such as eye fluttering, lip smacking, or body twitching. | There are no associated symptoms. |

## Treatment of ADHD and disorganization

Read Chapter 2 *"Read this Chapter! General principles of treatment"* All of Chapter 2 applies to ADHDers. Plan B will be of particular importance to parents. Go ahead and read it again. Really. We'll wait.

## Presenting material to ADHD children

- Clear the area of distractions.

- Present the material in a vibrant, animated, and attention-grabbing manner. ADHD kids will attend to whatever is most stimulating to them at the moment.

- Establish good eye contact. When asked, however, some children will be aware that eye contact actually interferes with their concentration. See what works best.

- Tap on the desk (or use another code) to bring the child back into focus.

- Alert the child's attention with directives such as, "This is important!"

- Break down longer directions into simpler chunks.

- Check for comprehension.

- Encourage students to underline the key words of directions.

- Encourage students to mark *incorrect* multiple-choice answers with an "x" first. This allows them to "get started" quickly, while forcing them to read all of the choices before making a final selection.

- Allow physically hyperactive children out of their seats to hand out and pick up papers, etc.

- Allow preferential seating. This is typically near the teacher, who is not always at the physical front of the classroom. For some children, though, being near the teacher means being near an overwhelming center of commotion. The preferred placement needs to be individualized, sometimes in direct discussion with the child.

## Helping with organization

*Recognize that disorganization is a major disability for almost everyone with ADHD.* In fact, the diagnostic criteria show that it is difficult to diagnose ADHD in the absence of organizational problems. Yes, ADHD students can—and frequently do—write a wonderful paper and then forget to hand it in. This striking unevenness in skills is what makes it a disability.

Keep plugging away at teaching organizational techniques, which are all based on *writing it down* somewhere else than in the child's inconsistent memory. Some children are fascinated enough by high-tech toys that they can use a palm computer (PDA—personal digital assistant). When the assignment pad isn't readily available, some kids manage to keep a piece of paper to scribble something on—and hopefully not lose it. For most students, though, a good organization system begins with the notebooks and assignment pads.

## NOTEBOOKS

Too many notebooks are confusing and too heavy. I have never met a parent who doesn't complain (when asked) about the use of so many notebooks. ADHD students should have the following:

- One notebook—a three-ring binder for all subjects. Ideally, no other binders! The student needs to date each sheet of paper as soon as he first touches it.

- One bi-fold homework folder for all subjects (one side for all papers coming home, the other for all papers to be handed in). Unless there is one central location for paperwork to be filed (or handed in), the ADHD child and his caregiver will never find it all.

- An assignment book. Make sure that they *use* it. Kids with ADHD often do not write in their planner. Please, come around and check for this student. If you check, you can be sure he gets practice using it. This will actually teach the skills, not just punish those that have not learned them. It's more productive—and easier—than dealing with the missed assignment. Always leave enough time at the end of class to write down the assignment—or give it before the end of class. ADHD kids will not write it down while running out, and the teacher will not have the opportunity to check it. Consider taping any weekly assignment sheets into the assignment book.

- A monthly calendar, which can be filled in by the whole school team, or just downloaded blank from the school website or www.timeanddate.com. Each monthly calendar must be provided well in advance of the first of the next month. In fact, all students could benefit from training and supervision in the use of a monthly calendar for longer-range projects. On the monthly calendar, indicate dates to break larger projects into smaller sections (such as finish the reading, writing the rough draft, editing, etc.).

## ASSIGNMENTS

Each day, the child and parent (and/or skills teacher) should look over the daily assignment pad as well as the monthly calendar of upcoming commitments and assignments. Any scraps of paper with notes on them should be rounded up and added to the list.

Next, convert the daily and monthly assignments into a time schedule for today. Look over the planner—including upcoming weeks—and write out the times that you are going to actually accomplish tasks today. This provides a reality check for what can and cannot be crammed into one day. Note that what you are planning to actually accomplish today may not correlate exactly with what is on today's assignment pad.

- Include time for eating, bathing, instant messaging, T.V., etc.

- Factor in time for unexpected delays—work taking too long, demands from parents, phone calls from friends, traffic jams, etc. The unexpected is expected.

- Adhere to the time schedule. This will help prevent taking diversions, since there is always an immediate deadline to meet.

- Caregiver and child should go over this time schedule as soon as the child makes it (which should be when coming home from school or in resource class). Children with ADHD typically have poor estimates of how long events will take. They will need our advice. Making this time schedule will allow them to see how well the estimates work out.

Until the child's organizational skills fully kick in—which likely will take just a few more decades—the teacher and parent will need to "lend" their own frontal lobes to the child. (When the ADHD children become adults, the wise ones will avail themselves of similar help from spouses and secretaries.) This involves both *teaching* the skill to use assignment pads, and *supervising* it. The day that the caregivers stop supervising the creation of this time map is likely to be the day it stops being done. Remember the concept of executive function.

Assignment pads are not helpful if they are not filled out correctly. Ensure that parents and child all know the correct assignment. Most students can take this responsibility upon themselves. Those with ADHD, though, usually cannot do it consistently. It is unfair and counterproductive to let intelligent students flounder because of this disability. Ask yourself: "Is the goal of this assignment to grade the kids on their ability to do physics and algebra; or are they being graded on their ability in an area of disability—to be self-organized?" Don't worry: the child is still responsible to get it done.

The following options can be used to keep the child (and parent) informed of the assignments. This part will take effort, especially to keep the system going:

- Inform about typical routines (such as quizzes every Friday).

- Hand out written assignments for the week.

- Put homework on the Internet or school website. Sites such as www.yourhomework.com offer free school homework pages, and require virtually no district administration setup or upkeep. Or use teacher voicemail for homework assignments.

- Initial students' homework assignment pads after each period. Please do not expect the students to come up after class for the signature on their own. If they were organized enough to do that, we would not need to provide this accommodation. And, yes, the typical student is organized enough to come to the teacher; but this is not the typical student.

- Practical experience shows that it is difficult to sustain a system of signing the homework pad. If unable to initial all new assignments, then be sure to use the other systems above, and to address any occasionally missed work as below.

Notify the family immediately of any late assignments. *This is key!* Waiting for a mid-term progress report is too late to correct the problem, and too late for the student to behaviorally notice the connection between his/her performance and the consequences. Use any of the following forms of communication:

- A phone call or e-mail takes the child out of the loop, and works best. E-mail is particularly useful because teachers are hard to reach during the day, and a brief e-mail note is certainly quicker than multiple missed phone call messages followed by an extended phone conversation.

- The parent could call the team leader/guidance counselor each week for an update.

- The parent could mail a card weekly to each teacher. The card would simply have spaces for missed work and comments, and is dropped back into the mail.

- A "Comment Book" can be transferred back and forth daily for comments between the teacher and parent.

Allow for expedient makeup of late homework. If deduction for lateness actually works to correct the problem, then keep doing it. If not, recognize the problem as a disability that is currently unable to be completely corrected. In such a case, the work does need to be completed, but is not fair for a persistent organizational disability to cause excessive and demoralizing deductions. Use one of two methods:

- Late work is accepted one day from direct parental notification.

- A non-punitive school detention can be assigned during which the work is done, and then accepted.

With either method, the student does all of the work (i.e., "gets away" with nothing), learns the material, and gets good grades. Without this support, the child "gets away" with not doing the work, does not learn the material, and gets bad grades. Isn't the more productive choice clear?

If, for some reason, it is necessary to give a failing grade for incomplete work, remember that 65% is failing, not 0%. Trying to get a decent quarterly grade while averaging in a "0%" or two is virtually impossible. For example, if a student gets four grades of 90% and just one 0%, her new average is 72%. Very demoralizing. A grade of "0%" is excessive, does not change the ADHDer's future behavior (it hasn't yet, has it?), and is actually counterproductive. From a purely mathematical perspective, even getting an extra five points for extra credit on some assignments can never compensate for losing 100 points on a missed one.

Another huge benefit of these approaches is that it allows the parent to back off a little. Without the fear of a major deduction for missed work, the parent does not have to micro-manage each and every assignment—scouring everything to find that occasional missed one. That degree of parental involvement is not typically well tolerated by a teen, especially one with the easy frustration threshold of ADHD.

### MORE SUPPORT TIPS

Some students benefit from two sets of books. A set of books for home, as well as a set of books to keep at school, will eliminate many stressful trips back to school to pick up textbooks.

Keep students and parents apprised of their grades.

- ADHD students often have an inflated sense of how well they are doing. A tangible record will allow a reality check for the child and parents.

- Consider giving a brief pre-test to allow for a reality test of their mastery *before* doing poorly on the test.

Use *tangible methods* to externalize problem areas.

- Explicitly state out loud the problem and consequences at the time of the event.

- Use timers and planners to break down tasks into manageable, concrete chunks. Timers give a tangible face to the nebulous concept of time, and will also help keep you from nagging.

- Brainstorm ideas on index cards or word processor. Then, physically sort through and put the topics in order.

Provide help for deficits at the moment it is needed, not negative feedback when it is already too late. Unfortunately, the simple reality is that punishment does not usually teach the needed behaviors to ADHD kids. The "sink or swim" approach works poorly with ADHD. Without enabling, they will keep sinking. That helps no one.

Use the resource room or a classroom aide to give skills support for classified children. Just teaching the skill a few dozen times to the ADHD student is not sufficient. After all, if it were sufficient, we would not still be considering these students for a skills program. The skills teacher should check organization skills daily.

- Check assignment sheet (which will need to be checked against web by skills teacher or parent; or, perhaps, check that a peer has initialed each assignment).

- Review books needed.

- Review due dates.

- Review plan for breaking down larger projects into steps.

- Review monthly calendar.

The skills teacher should also check for class notes for each subject in the binder daily. Printers may be needed in skills class for those students who take notes by computer.

*Keep it up.* Don't allow the success of organizational support to lead to its disuse. Once a program starts to work, then the problem "no longer exists," and everyone stops doing it. People may confuse the success of the program with the lack of need for it. ("Why should I check Johnny's homework when he hasn't missed any for weeks?") Unfortunately, the same problems will tend to reoccur as soon as the support is withdrawn.

## Medication treatment

In addition to the above, many children with ADHD benefit from medication. Often, medication will provide the basic neurological skills needed in order to comply with behavioral approaches. When prescribed for people who have ADHD, they stimulate the frontal parts of the brain that are not inhibiting ("filtering out") distractions as well as they should. The medications work in a similar way to caffeine. The children appear "calmer" because they are more focused, not because they are sedated.

Unfortunately, many people do not distinguish between stimulants and sedatives. An analogy may help. Imagine that ADHD people are like bicycles without brakes. Stimulants are analogous to giving the bike new brake linings—creating a higher functioning bike. Sedatives would be like pouring tar on the gears—creating a bike that is too tired to bother anyone. Indeed, pouring tar on the gears would be horrible; but creating a properly functioning system is appropriate. Then, we can ask the ADHD person to perform correctly.

Detailed information on medication is given in Chapter 14.

### FEEDBACK FOR PHYSICIANS (IF ON MEDICATION)

The largest multimodal treatment trial on ADHD showed that most community-based physicians do not provide optimal medication doses (Jensen, Hinshaw, Swanson, *et al.* 2001). Improved feedback from the schools would help identify areas where further improvement is still possible. Evaluations need to be done on a child's performance in different subjects at different times of the day. Teachers may submit:

- a published ADHD checklist (such as the Connor's checklist), which provides quick feedback

- a written brief paragraph on the child's progress by each teacher, which is probably at least as useful.

## "Will it all be okay?"

In summary, we miss the point when we address only the triad of inattention, impulsivity, and hyperactivity. These symptoms are only the tip of the iceberg. Much greater problems have usually been plaguing the child's life, but often no one has understood that the associated symptoms described above are part and parcel of the same neurologically based condition—or are from another part of the syndrome mix. Without this recognition, caregivers have thought that their ADHD child also was "incidentally" uncooperative and apparently self-absorbed. Unless we recognize that these extended symptoms are part of the same spectrum, teachers and parents will not mention them; and doctors will never deal with them.

Fortunately, the physical hyperactivity almost always resolves by middle school. We never see a 60-year-old man jump out of a shopping cart. Unfortunately, the other aspects of ADHD may persist into adulthood in about half of the children. Without the accompanying hyperactivity, it's easy to misinterpret the remaining symptoms as laziness or meanness. This is a particular problem during high school years.

Given all of this, it is reasonable to ask: "Will this go away?" Personally, I would rephrase the question as, "Will it be okay?" The answer can be "yes," but we must recognize that this is often the "50-year plan" of works in progress. In other words, these children can be wonderfully successful adults, while they continue to work on these issues over their lifetime. Meanwhile, we "just" need to patiently steer them in the positive direction. If we cannot keep their self-esteem up, though, then they will never productively use all of their energy when they become adults.

Finally, we must also keep in mind that some of the iceberg is fantastic and enviable. While the rest of us are obsessing about the future, or being morose about the past, people with ADHD are experiencing the present. ADHDers can be a lot of fun; dullness is never a problem. Their "why not?" attitude may free them to take chances that the rest of us may be afraid to take. Their flux of ideas may lead to creative innovations. And most importantly, their extreme passion can be a source of inspiration and accomplishment to the benefit of us all.

It's going to be quite a ride.

Chapter 4

# Learning Disabilities and Differences

Robert R. Wolff and Martin L. Kutscher

"If I'm so smart, how come I'm in *that* reading group?"

## Learning about learning disabilities
### What is "intelligence?"

What is "intelligence?" If forced to come up with a quick answer, most of us would reply, "I don't really know, but it's some kind of 'spark' that you either have or not."

However, there is no single spark that defines intelligence. Each of us has abilities in a multitude of different areas. We have separate sparks for the skills of reading (and to each of the multiple skills that go into that task), math, writing, spelling, music, art, sports, dancing, planning for the future, organization, being nice to people, saying "no" to drugs, street smarts, etc.

Even a person's "IQ" (intelligence quotient—by which most people mean the mathematically derived score on the WISC (Wechsler Intelligence Scale for Children) IQ test) actually samples ten to sixteen different kinds of intelligences—a set of intellectual skills needed to succeed in school. These tests are then just averaged to come up with a convenient but over-simplified single number. More details about the IQ are given at the end of this chapter.

The "spark" that is commonly considered most important in intelligence is the ability to make novel connections from previously unrelated data—a task often referred to as "creativity." We must remember, though, that this is just one of the tasks that a human being is required to do; and that even this skill of making novel connections varies depending on the subject area at hand.

## What is a "learning disability?"

All of us have some variation in our profile of these intellectual skills. For most of us, the profile would look like the rolling hills of New England. For a person with learning disabilities (LD), though, the profile would look more like the jagged Rocky Mountain landscape. Most of the skill areas are okay; but then, suddenly, a specific skill drops off of the cliff. The valleys may be identified as learning differences; or, if more severe, as learning disabilities. On the WISC, a difference of more than 15 points between the Performance IQ and the Verbal IQ typifies a learning disability.

To the neurologist, a student can be considered to have areas of learning difficulty and yet have no skill below grade average. For example, if a 5th grader generally performs at a 9th grade level, and his math skills are at the 6th grade level, then that child's math skills will hold back his other skills—even though his weakest area is still above average.

"Learning disability" implies an uneven learning profile. If the bulk of your sparks are below normal, then you are below normal intelligence or mentally retarded—although such people are often euphemistically labeled as LD. In addition, it is fair to add the requirement that a learning disability must significantly affect the child's functioning.

In short, being poor in the single skill of reading doesn't make you "stupid," any more than being great in the single skill of penmanship makes you a "genius." No one skill defines your intellect.

## Defining learning disabilities with big words

The U.S. federal government "legally" defines learning disabilities as follows:

> Specific learning disability means a disorder in one or more of the basic psychological processes involved in understanding or in

using language, spoken or written, which may manifest itself in an imperfect ability to listen, think, speak, read, write, spell, or to do mathematical calculations. The term includes such conditions as perceptual handicaps, brain injury, minimal brain dysfunction, dyslexia, and developmental aphasia. The term does not include children who have problems that are primarily the result of visual, hearing, or motor disabilities or mental retardation, emotional disturbance, or of environmental, cultural, or economic disadvantage. (Federal law 94-142, as amended in 1977 by the Individuals with Disabilities Education Disability Act)

Psychologists and school districts may have their own definitions, but the American Psychiatric Association "medically" defines four types of learning disabilities in the DSM-IV (APA 1994):

- LD in reading

- LD in mathematics

- LD in written expression

- LD not otherwise specified.

The diagnostic criteria for each of these can be summarized as:

- performance substantially below expectation

- resultant significant functional impairment

- difficulties exceed those expected with any associated sensory impairment.

There is also a separate developmental coordination disorder, in which difficulties with the skills of muscle control result in the impairment of the learning processes of writing, drawing, and sports. This disorder may be heralded by marked delays in achieving motor milestones (e.g. walking, crawling, sitting), dropping things, and "clumsiness."

Some authorities also consider the category of learning disabilities to include "communication disorders," which include receptive language problems, expressive language problems, and articulation disorders.

Dr. Betty Osman concludes that a learning disability is "a handicapping condition that interferes with the ability to store, process, or produce desired information." (Osman 1997, p.5)

Depending on the definition, estimates for the prevalence rate of LD in U.S. students are about 5% (e.g., Feinstein and Phillips 2004, p.352), with estimates ranging from 1% to 10%. Boys are affected more commonly than girls (except in math, where girls may predominate).

## When should learning disabilities be identified?

Clearly, learning disabilities should be identified as soon as possible. Early detection takes advantage of the brain's "plasticity," whereby the brain continues to lay down new neuronal pathways even after the child's birth. Early detection and treatment may also prevent problems with self-esteem and avoidance behaviors. Often, there are clues as early as preschool.

## Early warning signs

In general, signs of most learning disabilities will be evident by kindergarten or 1st grade. The first sign of a learning disability may be delayed development in speech and language skills. These problematic skills may be in receptive language, processing skills, expressive language, or verbal fluency. The child may have trouble with word recall (e.g., "You know, those things that we put on our hands when it's cold out.") There may be incorrect use of prepositions (e.g., "Get that yucky food *on* my plate!"). Children with delays in language processing may understand the individual words, but they come at them so quickly that much of the message is lost. Dr. Osman likens this to the experience of traveling through a foreign country with limited skills in that language (Osman 1997).

Often, learning disabilities will present as avoidance or a "lack of interest" in certain tasks. For example, kids with coordination problems may veer away from writing, coloring, or drawing tasks. All of us are naturally drawn to skills that we are good at, and avoid tasks that make us feel like poor performers.

It is doubtful that any child ever woke up and consciously decided to deliberately avoid a task—just for the pleasures of never developing that skill, getting poor grades, and of annoying their teachers. In short, consider the possibility of LD whenever you find yourself saying, "She isn't good at it because she doesn't practice." Poor reading skills are usually the root cause of reading avoidance—not vice versa.

## Impact of learning disabilities

Children with learning disabilities often suffer, both in the short term and long term.

In the short term, they may not even realize that they have a specific problem. All that they know is that they are not performing well in school. Certainly by 1st grade, children with LD are aware that they are not performing as well as their classmates. They can identify who is in the good reading group, and who is in the poor reading group.

Even if they are assured that it is just an isolated reading problem, they can still be heard to say, "If I'm so smart, how come I can't read?" The concept of individual sparks of intelligence is hard enough for us adults to understand, much less for a 1st grader.

LD kids are, in essence, doing poorly at their job (learning). Imagine how you would feel if you looked around and were doing the worst job of anybody at the office. Would you want to go to work? Imagine your frustration if you had the "Teflon syndrome," where learned material just did not stick. Teachers, themselves, may have a hard enough time handling the Teflon syndrome in their students. How would you handle it if you were just a little kid?

Loss of self-esteem from learning problems may lead to negative behaviors. The child may act out or become the class clown, and get sent to the principal's office. At least, there, he isn't having his nose rubbed in the fact that he cannot do the work. Getting sent out of class is remarkably effective in the short term, even if it is a horrendous long-term strategy. Remember, though, that children are not known for their foresight.

In the long run, LD is associated with the risk for multiple problems, such as:

- poor academic achievement

- poor self-esteem, depression, anxiety, alienation, and rebellion

- other neuropsychiatric conditions of the syndrome mix covered in this book, such as a 20% risk of attention deficit hyperactivity disorder (ADHD)

- delinquency

- dropping out of school

- substance abuse (one study found 24% of students with LD had a substance abuse disorder, vs. 9% of non-LD students: Feinstein and Phillips 2004)

- conduct disorder (85% of juvenile delinquents have received a diagnosis of LD: Feinstein and Phillips 2004).

Learning that life isn't always fair is a tough lesson.

Try some of the simulations of learning disabilities at our website www.PediatricNeurology.com/adhd2.htm. The frustration that you experience from these simulations may improve your empathy for the child with LD.

## Supporting the child with learning disabilities and differences
### General approaches

Academic skills are important, but they are only potential vehicles to a greater goal: a life filled with enough self-worth and happiness that you can help someone else reach those same goals of self-worth and happiness. Our goal as a child's caregivers is to maximize his potential as he moves along this path. Reading well is important; being happy and helpful is more important.

There are two basic strategies to help children move along this path:

- Strategies that "hammer away" at the area of deficit.

- Strategies that effectively circumvent it.

In dyslexia, for example, Orton-Gillingham (a structured, multisensory approach, stressing phonics grounded on language-based learning processes) is the hammer-away approach, whereas using books on tape is the circumvent approach. Both types of interventions have their essential and legitimate uses.

Dr. Osman points out that sometimes it might be better to consider learning disabilities as "learning differences." Reframing the "problem" as a "difference" causes us to seek alternate strengths that we can use to help overcome the weaknesses (Osman 1997, p.8). For example, if a child has an auditory processing problem, it is helpful to ask ourselves, "What *different* learning strategies would work?" In this case, we might remind ourselves that extensive use of the blackboard would help the child understand the material.

## Homework suggestions

In her book *Learning Disabilities and ADHD*, Dr. Betty Osman (1997) offers the following homework rules to be shared by teachers and parents:

1. Showing/helping a child with the homework is better than letting him agonize through it by himself. The child may really not have understood or paid attention to the class instruction. Agony that bears no fruit just leads to further avoidance.

2. For children with learning disabilities, it will typically take several explanations and reviews of the material to master it.

3. Break assignments into smaller pieces. For example, when reading a chapter, start by looking at the questions at the end, and find the answer to each question before reading the entire chapter. Many students still need to be taught how to study!

4. It is okay for the parent to be the secretary until the child becomes facile enough to handle the whole process by himself. (See the following section on use of word processors.)

5. Similarly, the parent may help a child by copying math problems if that proves to be the difficulty.

6. Make sure the student understands the directions *before* she does the work.

7. Start the first few problems together.

8. Pre-teach the material for the next day. Be aware, though, that many children are not interested in learning anything that is not required to enter class the next day. Dads, in particular, seem to need to keep this in mind.

9. Don't worry about the child becoming dependent on the parent as a crutch. Most children will give it up as soon as

they can. (More typically, parents have trouble getting the kid to accept the help in the first place.)

10. If a child accepts a parent's help, then fine. Otherwise, get outside help.

## Word processors

For many students with learning disabilities, ready access to a word processor is essential. The goal is to get the typist up and running quickly. Many students can start effective keyboarding by 3rd grade. There are many enticing computer games to learn typing at home. If possible, the child would ideally learn to use all ten fingers, but we'll settle for whatever works. It is okay if they look at their hands while typing. After all, there is no handwritten rough draft that they need to keep their eyes on. Once students have learned basic comfort on the keyboard, then homework and instant messaging will provide the needed practice.

The advantages of a word processor are numerous.

- It helps with dysgraphia, freeing the child's mind to focus on ideas rather than letter formations.

- Spellcheck and grammar-check are lifesavers. Don't worry—the child still has to decide which correct spelling to use. Let's just hope we can get them to look at those squiggly red and green lines.

- Learning to use a word processor is a life skill. There will be very little serious written work in a child's future that does not include one. All they really need to do by hand in the future is sign their name.

- Easy ability to make corrections will encourage the child to accept editing suggestions from the parent/teacher, since that does not mean copying the whole thing over.

- Easy future editing may make it easier for children with writer's block. Just start typing something. You can come back later for corrections.

- For pre-typists, parental use of a word processor lets the child focus on the more important aspects of the assignment. If a child has a writing problem, then consider having the child write what he can in the amount of time that the assignment is expected to take, and then let him dictate the rest to the parent. It is better to learn how to tell a creative story than it is to suffer through dysgraphia.

A few caveats on the use of computers:

- Elementary school teachers may be uncomfortable with the use of a word processor in class. The bell rings, the child runs out, and now the teacher is left feeling responsible for this expensive machine sitting in the middle of the classroom. In this setting, a good compromise is to allow the child to practice handwriting in class and typing at home.

- The school may consider a simple word-processing machine to be appropriate, rather than a full-fledged notebook computer.

- Students may feel stigmatized by the use of a word processor. This often resolves by secondary school. We can only push the child so far.

- The child's homework station should be equipped with its own computer and printer. It is not reasonable to expect a child with homework/ADHD problems to go back and forth between multiple work areas.

- No games or Internet connection should be on the child's laptop. They are much too distracting. Be aware that games seem to have their own mysterious habit of loading themselves onto a child's computer.

## Specific learning disabilities
### Reading disability ("dyslexia")

Dyslexia simply denotes abnormal reading. Although many people may focus on dyslexia as letter reversals, that does not need to be the case. A formal criteria for reading disability can be found in the DSM-IV (APA 1994) and has been summarized above. About 10% of children have some degree of dyslexia (Feinstein and Phillips 2004).

Of all learning disabilities, reading dysfunction has the most significant educational impact. Practically all subjects in school require reading proficiency, including math, word problems, and science.

## RISK FACTORS

Children with developmental expressive language disorders, articulation problems, or word retrieval deficits may be at particular risk for dyslexia. They may hear in their "mind's own ear" a different sound than the rest of us hear (by consensus) when we encounter written letters. Frequently, there is a family history of reading or academic problems.

Spontaneous spelling problems may also be a clue of an ongoing or residual reading problem. Formal spelling tests may go well; those are memory tests. However, the spelling problems appear during desk exercise or writing assignments. Some children with such spelling problems might still be effective readers, as much of reading involves contextual clues combined with the first and last few letters of a word. This ability was discovered at Cambridge University; you can demonstrate it to yourself with the following passage:

> Aoccdrnig to a rseearch at Cmabrigde Uinervtisy, it deosn't mttaer in what order the ltteers in a wrod are, the only iprmoatnt thing is that the frist and lsat ltteer be in the rghit pclae. The rset can be a total mses and you can still raed it wouthit a porbelm. This is beuscae the human mind deos not raed ervey lteter by istlef, but the word as a wlhoe.

Amazing, huh?

## STEPS INVOLVED IN READING

In order to understand dyslexia, we need to consider the steps in reading, which include:

- decoding
- comprehension
- retention.

□ *Decoding* is the first step. Research clearly shows that phonological dysfunction appears to be the root problem for most people with dyslexia. Trouble attaching names to letters in kindergarten, and trouble attaching sounds to letters by late kindergarten/early 1st grade, are huge red flags of underlying problems. Early phonologic problems are a prelude to reading difficulties, and should trigger a referral for assessment.

Children also learn to read from visual memory—another potential problem area in dyslexia. Students with dyslexia may not remember the visual experience of the word from one page to the next—sight words may not "stick." Perceptual problems may also include letter reversals (which resolve in the non-LD child by age 7 years). Additionally, the child might find that the words move, glare, or jump around.

"Visual tracking," though, is *not* felt to be a problem in dyslexia. Most objective authorities agree that visual exercises are of no help in dyslexia, and may take time away from other more effective strategies.

☐ *Reading comprehension* problems may be due to early decoding problems, but can occur with or without reading decoding problems. The child might whizz through the passage, but have no clue as to its literal or deeper meaning. They might gloss over important details, may be unable to distinguish important from unimportant facts, may not be able to see the connections between facts, or simply not understand words or sentences.

☐ *Retention problems* may also exist. By 3rd grade, "reading to learn" (versus "learning to read," which is the focus of early elementary years) is an essential part of amassing information. Early signs of reading retention problems include trouble recalling or summarizing what was just read, or connecting it to previous knowledge or personal experiences.

### IMPORTANCE OF EARLY DETECTION AND AGGRESSIVE TREATMENT

A series of review articles (Torgesen 2004; Wattenberg 2004) in the Fall 2004 issue of *American Educator* (the quarterly journal of the American Federation of Teachers) makes the following essential points:

- The "late bloomer" theory of reading lag is officially dead; 88% of poor readers at the end of 1st grade will still be poor readers at the end of 4th grade—unless there is early, aggressive intervention.

- Reading problems are typically due to deficits in phonics skills.

- Left to their own devices, poor readers will fall further behind.
  - Poor, inconsistent decoding skills hinder development of essential sight-word recognition. Good readers develop a much larger library of sight-words than do poor readers.
  - Poor decoding skills means poor vocabulary development.
  - Poor decoding skills lead to poor comprehension skills.
  - All of the above lead to lack of practice in reading—by just the children who actually need extra practice.

- Recognize the red flags of reading problems. According to Schatschneider and Torgesen (2004), the following problems should lead to further evaluation, monitoring, and likely treatment:
  - Failure to know the names of letters by early kindergarten.
  - Failure to know the sounds of letters by late kindergarten.
  - Trouble with decoding and reading fluency by the second part of 1st grade.

- Early detection is essential. In fact, research suggests that students from kindergarten to 3rd grade should be repeatedly screened formally and informally.

- Aggressive and early treatment is successful for most children. Depending on the particular study of early, intensive intervention, 56 to 92% of poor readers have been brought into the average range. This hopefully includes starting by kindergarten and 1st grade.

- Early intervention is much more successful than later treatment.

- Children identified at-risk for reading problems need reading instruction that is:
  - *more explicit* than for other students. (No decoding skill can be taken for granted. The connection between a letter and its sound should be taught in a comprehensive fashion. Words and their associated meanings need to be explicitly taught.)
  - *more intensive* than for other students. (Typically, this would mean time in small groups.)
  - *more supportive* than for other students. (The appropriate scaffolding of basic skills needs to be steady before taking on the next step. Positive reinforcement is essential.)

The above general guidelines may need to be adjusted to the individual child and school district. It is important to note that each state and district has its own teaching style mandates.

## TREATMENT APPROACHES

The classroom teacher can use the following suggestions to supplement the additional individualized interventions. Not every student learns the same way. Most teachers will employ a variety of reading strategies for the students to use.

- Phonics will be essential for the poor decoder. We cannot assume that everyone can teach themselves the rules of phonics.

- Sight-word recognition should be taught for words that do not follow the phonic rules, and for speed.

- Whole-language, which stresses meaning, literature, and language, is a widely used approach. However, at least some (if not all) students in a class will either benefit from or completely require use of the other strategies.

The following list of suggestions for helping students with reading problems is largely inspired by Dr. Kenneth Shore's excellent book *Special Kids Problem Solver* (2002) (see Further Reading).

- If a child does not read very often, check if there is a problem. Ask the child to read for you in private. Can he read phonetically, blend sounds, and comprehend what he read? When in doubt, have the child checked by the school's reading specialist. Formal and informal screenings are ideally repeated through the early school years.

- Teach phonics, starting at the beginning if needed. You may need to start over with letter formation, letter sounds, and blending sounds. Use materials that allow these skills to be practiced in the context of *meaningful* material. This will often require a small group setting.

- Provide individualized sessions for special need students to go over the material.

- Reading, reading, everywhere. Point out that words are everywhere: T-shirts, greeting cards, signs, posters, magazines, and books. Have books of all levels and many areas of interest easily accessible in the room. Try to have material of interest to the child.

- Give reading material at a level that encourages a sense of mastery. In order for a text to be enjoyable, the child should be able to read at least 90% of the words with relative ease. Give material based on the child's ability, not his chronological age. Re-reading material adds to the sense of success. *Do not frustrate the child!*

- Use multisensory approaches. Have the student say the letter while drawing it with his finger in the air, in the sand, in his mind, or in finger-paint. The goal is to see, hear, and touch the letters.

- Encourage the child to visualize the scene that the words describe.

- Teach to sight read commonly used words. This will speed up reading. The first 100 words of Fry's Instant Word List make up 50% of a student's reading. These words can be placed on a "word wall," and practiced five words/week. Download the list from www.makereadingfirst.com/word_list.pdf.

- Lessen the stress of reading out loud. Allow the student to practice the passage in advance, do not correct minor mistakes, and make sure no one ever criticizes. If necessary, allow the student to skip this task.

- Utilize books on tape to familiarize the child with the material he will read.

- Keep reading to the child. Let them know that is great stuff waiting in all of those books.

- Teach and model comprehension strategies, such as how to:
  - pre-read the text quickly; this allows the student to know where the text is going, and gives a framework upon which to hang the new information
  - make predictions about what will happen next
  - convert textbook topic headings into questions. For example, change the topic heading "The Causes of World War II" into the question, "What were the causes of WWII?" Now, you are reading that section with a purpose
  - ask yourself questions about what you just read
  - monitor your own comprehension, to determine when you need to slow down or re-read a passage
  - summarize what you just read
  - read out loud, if needed, to help comprehension (although that certainly slows reading).

- Provide reading aid in advance, for example:
  - go over difficult words in the passage
  - give a summary, or even an outline
  - construct a visual map of the information to show how it all connects.

- DEAR (Drop Everything And Read) time. Give the class 20 minutes per day of high-priority, uninterrupted silent reading time. Make it a daily highlight and treat.

- Encourage parents to read to their young child every day. Make it a special time.

- Work with the school reading specialist or psychologist.

- Consider accommodations, for example:
  - shorten length of assignment
  - equip with notes from the teacher, a peer, or a scribe
  - oral exams
  - use of laptop for spelling
  - extra time.

- Keep it fun!

## Mathematics disorder

Early signs of a mathematics disorder include difficulty with sorting items by shape or size, or matching numbers with quantities. Typical children learn their early math calculations with visual reinforcement, such as counting fingers, but become less reliant on these as they practice. Children with a math disorder, though, may experience the Teflon effect as they try to master simple addition and subtraction—no less with multiplication, division, or algebra. Despite repetition, it is harder for them to make math facts automatic. Mathematics disorder also may include problems with perceptual or mathematical concepts.

The disorder occurs in 5% to 6% of school age children (Shalev 2004). Some, but not all, studies show predominance amongst girls.

### TREATMENT APPROACHES

The following recommendations are largely based on Dr. Kate Garnett's article *Math Learning Disabilities* (1998) which can be found at www.ldonline.org.

Trouble with basic number facts:

- Give intensive practice, with materials that gain the student's attention. Use games that motivate children to actually pay attention to their practice.

- Distribute practice into multiple, short sessions (about 15 minutes each?).

- Master small groups of calculations at a time. Then mix the different groups.

- Emphasize that there are many of the same problems that are just in a different order ($2\times3 = 3\times2$).

- Teach special sets of problems, such as 5+5, 6+6, 7+7; or 5+6, 6+7, 7+8...

- Use accommodative strategies:
  - Use a calculator.
  - Use personal math fact summary charts (pocket sized). Block off answers as they are mastered.

- Keep a child who has good math concepts in a stimulating math tract, while simultaneously acknowledging and treating specific problem areas.

Trouble understanding mathematical symbols:

- Use concrete manipulatives along with the graphical symbols. Learning the meaning of symbols such as "–" can be difficult even for a child who naturally understands the concept of subtraction.

Trouble with the verbal parts involved in math:

- Break instructions into small chunks.

- Give instructions slowly.

- Have students explain the math process to themselves or to others. Having the student teach the process helps to clarify and integrate the material.

- Have students self-verbalize what the problem is asking them to do.

Trouble with the visual-spatial parts of math—compensate by using words or manipulatives:

- Use words to describe what most of us "see." For example, most of us see something with three sides and instantly visually recognize it as a triangle. Students with visual-spatial problems may need to be told (or say to themselves): "I have counted three sides. That makes this a triangle."

- Teach the child to talk himself through each step of a problem.

- Use verbal constructs (words!) rather than diagrams.

- Supplement instruction with concrete manipulatives.

Trouble with the graphomotor parts of math:

- Use graph paper to line up problems.

- Encourage students to show their work in a vertical fashion, with each step shown below the previous step.

- Use lots and lots of space on handouts/homework. Don't cram it all into tiny spaces on one page. This is no time to save trees.

## Writing disorder

Writing disorders are marked by difficulties with punctuation, grammar, spelling, organization, and handwriting. Handwriting itself requires an orchestration of a remarkably complex sequence of movements. Writing disorders occur in some 2% to 8% of children, predominantly in boys (Feinstein and Phillips 2004). Usually, it occurs in combination with other disabilities, such as developmental coordination disorder.

### TREATMENT APPROACHES

- Liberal use of a laptop. See the section on use of computers (p.68).

- Give extra points for neatness, but minimize deductions for messiness (i.e., keep it positive).

- Provide the student with alternate ways of getting notes: a copy of a peer's notes, a copy of the teacher's notes, or a scribe.

- Consider referral to occupational therapy for handwriting problems.

- Teach how to organize thoughts—utilizing graphic organizers, sorting index cards, outlining, etc.

- Give exams orally, or allow use of a scribe. Remember: Is the goal of this particular test to check, for example, a student's knowledge of photosynthesis, or is the goal to test writing skills. (Yes, in most students, we want to teach and test both subject knowledge and writing skills, but this is not the typical student.)

## Developmental coordination disorder

Developmental coordination disorder—unskillful or clumsy performance of sequential motor skills—is defined formally by the DSM-IV (APA 1994). This disorder potentially shares handwriting/pencil grip problems (dysgraphia) with writing disorder, but focuses on a broader problem with muscle skills. Children with this disorder may present with developmental motor problems (gross or fine motor). It occurs in 6% of school age children (Feinstein and Phillips 2004).

While motor coordination problems are not usually considered as typical learning disabilities, they are included here because:

- like learning disabilities, they are isolated skill areas that are poor compared to the child's other skills

- problems in this area can inhibit learning in other areas

- some of the children with typical learning disabilities also have motor control issues and vice versa.

### DEVELOPMENTAL COORDINATION DISORDER VS. CEREBRAL PALSY

The degree to which muscle coordination is affected determines the diagnosis of a developmental coordination disorder versus cerebral palsy (CP). While both terms refer to a deficit in motor (muscle) functioning, cerebral palsy is identified by its greater degree of severity, and associated "hard" findings on neurological examination. In contrast, a coordination disorder denotes a far milder degree of dysfunction, without classic neurological abnormalities.

In CP, there is something wrong with the control exerted by the brain over the child's muscles. By definition, it does not start with a problem within the muscles themselves. In fact, the scientific name for CP is "static motor encephalopathy," which means just what it says: a non-progressive (static) problem of muscle control (motor) due to a brain problem (encephalopathy). Even within the domain of "cerebral palsy" there is a spectrum, ranging from mild to profoundly severe. The term cerebral palsy certainly does not connote mental retardation, although the two conditions may frequently co-exist.

The term "cerebral palsy" does not convey a specific cause of the problem. Most cases of CP are related to prenatal factors occurring well before the time of birth, which are still not well understood. Despite significant advances that have taken place in prenatal and perinatal medicine over the last few decades, the incidence of CP has remained largely unchanged.

Most children with CP have developmental motor delays that present themselves in later infancy—often by 8–10 months of age. Early handedness may be an initial marker. Handedness (righty vs. lefty) is usually not developed until approximately two years of age. Thus, for example, a clear right-handed preference at one year of age may imply a motor deficit on the left side of the body (right brain).

There are different patterns of CP. Neurologists distinguish between them with terms such as paraparesis, tetraplegia, hemiparesis, and extrapyramidal. The suffix –plegia implies a more severely affected state than –paresis, which suggests a milder or incomplete form.

- *Paraparesis* means that a child has symptoms in both legs. The legs may show spasticity—where the muscles tighten up, especially when they are moved suddenly. Such children may walk late and be toe-walkers. Paraparesis is a common finding in children who were born very prematurely.

- *Quadriplegia (tetraplegia)* is a more severe form of CP in which all four extremities are involved. These children have poor coordination involving not just the legs, but of their arms, hands, fingers, and perhaps oral motor movements including expressive speech as well. Many of these children are wheelchair bound. They have a higher incidence of seizures and mental retardation. Computer-assisted technology evaluations can help greatly.

□ *Hemiparesis (or hemiplegia)* affects either the entire right or left side of the body. A left hemiparesis implicates a right cerebral hemisphere disturbance, and vice versa. In most children, there is an identifiable cause that can be visualized on modern imaging studies. Again, there are different degrees of impairment seen, from mild to severe. Unlike in adults, whose nervous system is fully developed, cerebral hemispheric impairments in children tend to have less predictable effects upon cognition. Typically, children with left hemispheric damage (right hemiparesis) may have more deficits involving verbal skills and discerning detail. Children with right hemispheric damage tend to have problems with spatial reasoning and getting the gestalt, especially of visually presented material.

□ *Hypotonic* children have low muscle tone. They may first present as "floppy" infants. Hypotonic cerebral palsy implies a greater degree of neurological dysfunction than the term developmental coordination disorder.

□ *Extrapyramidal* cerebral palsy refers to disturbances of motor posture (dystonic); or peculiar slow, writhing movements of the arms/legs in an involuntary fashion (athetoid); or to a disconnected, purposeless rapid movement about the arms, trunk, hands, and tongue (choreiform). This type of CP is much less common.

### TREATMENT OF MOTOR COORDINATION PROBLEMS

Early intervention with multiple services may significantly reduce later dysfunction, by taking advantage of a child's ability to form new neuronal circuits.

- Consider occupational therapy referral for hand/fine motor problems.

- Consider physical therapy referral for leg/gross motor problems.

- Treat secondary emotional problems. Children with CP are at a high risk for self-esteem, anxiety, and mood problems. Many children with significant ambulation issues can become extremely anxious, especially in busy classroom setting. Those children with CP who have normal cognition typically first become aware of their disabilities in their sixth year.

See also sections on word processors (p.68) and writing disorders (p.78)

## Mental retardation

Mental retardation (MR) is the term applied when most of a person's individual sparks are well below average. There may still be variations; but overall, most intellectual skills are poor. There may sometimes be additional muscle control problems, but they are not considered part of MR, per se. Three out of every 100 people has retardation; and in most of these individuals, the degree of retardation is mild (Szymanski and Kaplan 2004). Children with autistic spectrum disorder have a higher incidence of retardation, but are particularly likely to have extreme variations in their different cognitive skills.

### WHAT IS "IQ"?

More formally, MR is quantified by IQ, which stands for intelligence quotient.

$$IQ = \frac{\text{intellectual age}}{\text{chronological age}} \quad \text{(expressed as percent)}$$

For example, if a 10-year-old child functions intellectually at the 6-year-old level, then his $IQ = 6/10 = 60\% = $ "60."

There are a number of IQ tests, of which we most commonly mean the Wechsler Intelligence Scale (WISC). The WISC-3 actually samples ten areas of intelligence, plus an optional coding test. Five of these WISC-3 subscales are averaged together to form the Verbal IQ (VIQ), and the five other subscales are averaged to form the Performance IQ (PIQ). The VIQ and PIQ are averaged together to come up with the Full Scale IQ (FSIQ).

The newer WISC-IV examination consists of 16 subtests, which are grouped together to derive four scores—Verbal, Perceptual, Memory, and Processing Speed. The WISC-IV has norms for children of different groups, such as ADHD, Asperger's, etc.

A *"normal"* IQ is considered to be in the range of 90–110, with an IQ of 100 being perfectly average for age. The *"mental retardation"* range IQ is defined as more than two standard deviations below the norm, i.e., IQ <70. The standard deviation is 15 points. A *"borderline zone"* IQ is between 70 and 80. The first clue of a mildly low IQ is typically poor academic performance in the early primary grades. Assessment and identification are critical to determine special needs. Such children may benefit greatly from specifically directed vocational programs in secondary school.

### DSM-IV CRITERIA FOR MENTAL RETARDATION

Here are greatly simplified medical DSM criteria for mental retardation:

- significantly sub-average intellectual functioning—an IQ of approximately 70 or below

- trouble with functioning in multiple areas of life

- onset before age 18.

DSM-IV uses the full-scale IQ to define the following subcategories:

☐ *Mild MR*—IQ range of 50–55 to approximately 70. Represents the vast majority of people with MR. Such children typically reach a 6th grade level by their late teens.

☐ *Moderate MR*—IQ range of 35–40 to 50–55.

☐ *Severe MR*—IQ range of 20–25 to 35–40.

☐ *Profound MR*—IQ below 20–25. These more severely affected children are more likely to have a diagnosable neurological problem. There is an increased risk for seizures, motor impairments, communication deficits; as well as psychiatric disorders including anxiety, mood disturbances, and psychosis.

## THE EDUCATION PROCESS FOR CHILDREN WITH MR

Children with mild retardation usually appear normal initially, and have normal acquisition of gross motor and fine motor milestones; but usually show some delay in comprehending verbal concepts or immaturity of behavior. The condition is often not first appreciated until approximately four to six years of age, when they appear to be slow in processing information, and seem less capable than their peers in coping with academic challenges. Psycho-educational testing should be done for any child where such a suspicion exists in order to determine the appropriate education placement.

The education of retarded children requires a high degree of individual commitment, patience, willingness to provide emotional support, and constant repetition. Fortunately, the last several decades have witnessed a quiet but positive revolution in the care of such individuals. In contrast to the massive "warehouses" that existed for the mentally disabled not that many years ago, such children are cared for at home. Services such as speech therapy, occupational therapy, cognitive therapy, and physical therapy are now largely under the auspices of preschool, and school programs.

Inclusion programs, in which children are placed in a mainstream classroom regardless of their disability, present a particular challenge to teachers and students alike. The benefit of this controversial but widely practiced educational experiment has yet to be determined.

The educational process for MR children requires an emphasis on training for pragmatic life skills. Unfortunately, children with retardation rarely acquire the ability to achieve independent citizenship. Being able to balance a checkbook, read a tax form, or arrange for a mortgage may be simply beyond their capacities. They will require ongoing support services throughout life, some to a much greater degree than others.

## Chapter 5

# Autistic Spectrum Disorders: An Overview

Great, you figured something out. Congratulations! Now, you *may* want to share that idea with another human mind. If so, your brain translates the idea into a sequence of words. The words are translated into vibrations that depart from your mouth, sail long distances through the air, and land on my eardrum. These vibrations are turned back into words, and then into meaningful sentences and ideas. My brain also picks up other non-verbal language, such as your facial expression and tone of voice. Meanwhile, I figure out any "hidden agenda" or "subtext" when you said those words. All of these elements mix together to come up with an accurate understanding of what your "self" meant to communicate to my "self."

In this chapter "communication" is used in the broadest possible sense—including spoken speech, non-verbal clues, social skills, and the ability to use imagination and symbolic representations.

With this much involved, it's amazing that humans can communicate fully at all. It is not really amazing that some people have trouble with some aspect of the process. Given all of the ways that communication can go awry, this is a complex topic.

First, we'll start with a discussion of the underlying skills involved in communication, and then move on to the actual disorders. As we pull together a lot of essential information, we'll try to demystify technical terms. Hold on to your hats!

## Skills involved in communication

Communication involves two broad areas: *literal verbal skills*, and *non-verbal skills*. People with an autistic spectrum disorder (ASD) have problems that include (at a minimum) the non-verbal areas—including difficulty with their desire and ability to use language in a social context. Let's examine these categories of communication skills in more detail.

### Literal verbal/spoken communication skills

*Semantic language* refers to the ability to use and understand words, phrases and sentences; including abstract concepts and idioms. These skills involved in the literal use of verbal language may or may not be affected in ASDs. The skills needed for semantic language include the following:

☐ *Receptive verbal language*—the ability to *understand* spoken/written words and ideas. Central auditory processing (CAP) is used to get meaning from sounds and words. Such skills include the ability to distinguish between similar sounds, and to pick out the main voice from the background. CAP is covered in Chapter 13.

☐ *Expressive verbal language*—the ability to *express* our ideas with spoken/written words, including the ability to articulate each word clearly.

### Non-verbal/non-spoken communication skills

By definition, people with ASD have problems in the non-verbal/non-spoken areas of communication.

Let's explain non-verbal communication by way of analogy. Imagine that a typical three-year-old, English-speaking child is parachuted into Russia. Some Russian women—who don't speak any English—find him on the farm. Even though they would not understand any words from each other, they would be able to have a great deal of communication. The child could let the women know that he was scared and hungry. The women could let him know that he was welcome, and that they'd take care of him. All of this would happen without words. It is just like if you go to a restaurant in a foreign country—everyone would know that you were enjoying the experience, even without your saying it. Such is the power of non-verbal communication.

The communicative skills that are still available to the parachuted child in a foreign country are the areas that are weak in a child with an ASD. These skills include:

- the urge to initiate shared social interaction and two-way communication: theory of mind

- pragmatic language

- knowledge of unwritten rules

- knowing what is and isn't important

- symbolic play skills

- the ability to achieve "joint attention"

- non-verbal (non-spoken) transmission of language.

### URGE TO INITIATE SHARED SOCIAL INTERACTION AND TWO-WAY COMMUNICATION: THEORY OF MIND

The ability to socialize/relate/empathize requires a working "theory of mind." Theory of mind refers to the relatively unique ability of humans to understand: that I have a mind; that you have a mind; and most importantly, that our minds may not know or be feeling the same things. Without a theory of mind, there is little point in communicating. There is limited ability to truly recognize that there is another human being in the room. It will be difficult to feel the need to communicate with anyone else. After all, with whom would you be communicating? Eye contact will be poor. It may seem as if there is a pane of glass between the child and others.

With limited ability to "get inside your mind," it will be frequently difficult for the child to demonstrate empathy for what you are feeling. For example, a child with theory of mind problems may assume that since he is happy, then you must be happy; or the child may not understand that someone else is deceptive when he is always bluntly honest.

Thus, the ability to recognize that other people have a mind, the ability to relate to that mind, and the ability to empathize with that mind are all parts of the same skill. Theory of mind problems may underlie many of the difficulties seen in the autistic spectrum disorders.

Closely related to this "*interest*" in social communication (that arises from a working theory of mind) is the *ability* to communicate socially. The skills discussed below are required to actually achieve the meaningful interaction. Certainly, if you don't have these required skills, your interest in social interaction may appear blunted.

### PRAGMATIC LANGUAGE

Pragmatic language is the practical ability to use language in a social setting, such as knowing what is appropriate to say, where and when to say it; and the give and take nature of conversation. Effective pragmatics requires a working theory of mind: the ability to figure out what the other person does or does not already know—or might or might not be interested in hearing about. Examples of pragmatic language/theory of mind problems would be:

- A new student moves into the school district and enters the classroom for the first time. The teacher asks him where he comes from. The autistic spectrum child responds: "From the hallway."

- As an Asperger's child walks into the office, the doctor notices that her pink shirt matches the color of her jacket. He jokes, "If you change into a green shirt, does the color of the jacket change, too?" The child responds: "My wardrobe includes a turquoise shirt, not a green one." This child's spoken language is precise, but she misses the actual meaning of the question; and, more importantly, that the whole purpose of this conversation was just a little fun chit-chat to initiate an interaction.

## KNOWLEDGE OF UNWRITTEN RULES

There is an incredible array of essential social norms that most typical children do not need to be explicitly taught. Did your mother have to tell you to look at people when you talk to them? Did your mother have to teach you how close to stand to someone? Did your mother have to teach you how to read facial expressions?

Liane Holliday Willey describes her own frustrating experience with Asperger's as follows:

> I never got the hang of it. For example, I can never tell how much time should pass before I buy for someone I just met a "thinking of you gift." Do I really have to talk on the phone to anyone if I think the conversation is boring or a waste of my time? If there is a lapse in the conversation, am I supposed to hang up or tell a joke or just sit there? What if I like the person well enough, but I decide I cannot stand one of their behaviors or habits? The questions are endless, and the concerns are mountain high. This is why human relationships usually take me beyond my limits. They wear me out. (Willey 1999, p.55)

As a quick rule of thumb, whenever you find yourself saying, "I shouldn't have to tell you that…," consider that you might be dealing with an ASD symptom.

## KNOWING WHAT IS AND ISN'T IMPORTANT

The skills to know what is—and what is not—important include:

- the ability to see the big picture rather than fixate on details
- the ability to maintain a full range of interests.

## SYMBOLIC PLAY SKILLS

Give a child a yellow box on wheels, with thin long black stripes on it. The ability to understand that this object actually represents a school bus is a type of communication. Speech pathologist Elaine Schneider points out that, if a child cannot even recognize that a physical toy bus stands for a real bus, how will he be able to recognize later that the graphic letters "B-U-S" represents a bus, too? Both involve the use of symbols rather than the actual object to communicate (Schneider, verbal communication 2005).

By 18 months, most toddlers start to use objects as symbols for something else. For example, a cup is for drinking, but it also makes quite a handy telephone. By three years of age, most children are quite good at "let's pretend" activities, such as "You be the cowboy!" The toy school bus is not fascinating because the cold metal box can move, but because little toy figures chat while getting on it as they go to school. Stuffed animals are not just warm rags of cloth to drag around, but appear to be living creatures that have feelings and needs such as to be fed, dressed, and loved.

So, by 18–36 months of age, typical children make continuous progress in the skill of appreciating the representational meaning of a toy, rather than focusing on its straightforward physical attributes. Failure to develop representational/symbolic/pretend play is a strong marker of the autistic spectrum disorders.

### ABILITY TO ACHIEVE "JOINT ATTENTION"

A really cool limousine passes by. The child excitedly points to it, so that you can share in the experience with him. This important form of social communication is called "joint attention"—you are jointly sharing the same experience. Note that he isn't pointing simply to use you as a mechanical tool, such as pointing to the refrigerator so that you will satisfy his thirst for milk. Delayed ability to point for joint attention may be a marker for an ASD, even before delayed speech is noticed.

### NON-VERBAL (NON-SPOKEN) TRANSMISSION OF LANGUAGE

The simple sounds are not the only thing my body sends through space when it attempts to communicate with you. It also transmits:

- facial expressions
- body language
- tone and prosody (rhythm) of speech.

## Secondary problems resulting from failure to understand

If the child does not understand what is going on around her—especially if pragmatic/socialization cues are difficult—secondary problems usually occur in the autistic spectrum disorders. The child will frequently appear:

- *anxious*, since she doesn't know what she is supposed to do, or where the next blunder will come from

- *insistent on sameness* and showing ritualistic behavior. Change means that previously hard-learned strategies will not help in this situation. These kids are barely hanging on. One new wrinkle can throw them over the edge. For example, Jill may know that her first task each day is to take her lunch out of the backpack. What happens, though, if today there is only half a day of school, and the lunch is missing? Now what does she do? The child may be unraveled for the rest of the day

- *inattentive*, since it's hard to pay attention to something she does not understand

- *rude*, since she doesn't understand rules of conversation such as waiting your turn

- *interested in objects rather than people*; after all, objects are more predictable

- *"hanging back"* from peers, for all of the above reasons, and from simply not knowing how to make conversation and relate

- *"out of it"* and "odd" looking

- *socially unwelcome*. This can become quite painful, especially as the child gets older. Says Holliday Willey, "To choose to be left out is one thing, but to be locked out is quite another…I was crippled when I found out that it took more than I had to give to make new friends." (Willey 1999, p.72)

## Categories of communication disorders: sorting them out

When a child has difficulties in these areas out of proportion to his/her general cognitive abilities, he/she can be considered to have a communication disorder.

Difficulties in the above skills can group together in varying combinations and severities, allowing for the naming of several communication disorder syndromes. As we shall see, these disorders overlap greatly. Some may even be duplicates of the same condition but approached by different specialties. Additionally, as children develop, their diagnostic classification might change. The human brain is not so simple that its disorders fit into neat, static categories. Nonetheless, we still attempt to find certain patterns. Unless we know about the range of syndromes, we will fail to look for important symptoms that need to be addressed.

Disorders of the communication skills are grouped into two major types of disorders. Let's give an overview of the organizational scheme first, and then come back to each condition in detail later.

☐ *Typical language-based learning disorders* are due to problems in the purely spoken/written language communication skills. These include expressive, receptive, processing, and articulation language disorders. Most routine speech and language evaluations examine these areas. Note that routine psychological testing (such as the WISC "IQ" —Wechsler Intelligence Scale for Children) examines areas of cognition (thinking), rather than language per se.

☐ *Autistic spectrum disorders (ASD)* are those that include non-spoken communication problems—in particular, problems with socialization/empathy. In other words, the autistic spectrum disorders all share trouble with theory of mind, socialization, the pragmatics of language, and representational play. They may occur with or without additional verbal speech problems.

In turn, the autistic spectrum disorders are written about in two groupings:

- pervasive developmental disorders
- other autistic spectrum disorders.

The *pervasive developmental disorders* (PDDs), defined medically in DSM-IV by the American Psychiatric Association, are a series of five diagnoses, of which autistic disorder is the most commonly discussed. "Pervasive" means that the problem cuts across multiple types of communication. Note that "PDD" is technically an overlying category for a group of actual individual specific diagnoses. So, it is better to talk of "the PDDs." These five PDDs are:

- *autistic disorder*—severely disordered verbal *and* non-verbal language; unusual behaviors; commonly referred to as "autism"

- *Asperger's syndrome*—relatively good verbal language, with "milder" non-verbal language problems; restricted range of interests and relatedness

- *PDD-NOS* (not otherwise specified)—non-verbal language problems not meeting strict criteria for other PDD disorders

- *Rett's disorder*—rare neurodegenerative disorder of girls

- *childhood disintegrative disorder*—a rare disorder that needs to be carefully distinguished from a neurodegenerative condition.

Meanwhile, the rest of the world has extended the spectrum beyond those conditions discussed in DSM-IV to include *other autistic spectrum disorders*. To date, these terms have not been formally integrated into DSM-IV vocabulary. Presumably, they are subsumed under the category of PDD-NOS. In summary, these include:

- *high-functioning autism*—for some authors, synonymous with Asperger's; for others, implies milder autism without retardation

- *non-verbal learning disabilities*—trouble integrating information in three areas: non-verbal difficulties causing the child to miss the major gestalt in language; spatial perception problems; and motor coordination problems

- *semantic-pragmatic language disorder*—delay and trouble with the use of language (both semantic and pragmatic), but socialization relatively spared

- *hyperlexia*—most notable for incredible rote reading skills starting at an early age

□ *some aspects of ADHD* (attention deficit hyperactivity disorder)—the impulsivity and self-control difficulties in ADHD may cause kids to have trouble showing their empathy.

## DSM-IV pervasive developmental disorders

We start our more detailed review of each autistic spectrum disorder by presenting a summary of the key diagnostic criteria for each of the five PDD disorders as defined in DSM-IV (APA 1994).

### AUTISTIC DISORDER

By DSM-IV criteria, children with autistic disorder must have problems in each of the following three areas:

1. *Social interaction problems.* There are significant problems with non-verbal communication like body language, eye contact, and facial expressions. Peer relationships are inadequate, and the child has trouble returning emotions during interactions. The person does not seek to share achievements or interests via pointing or bringing things for praise.

2. *Communication problems.* There are significant spoken language problems (which are not compensated by signing). The person has trouble keeping up or starting a conversation (in those children who can speak). The speech tends to be stereotyped and/or repetitive. There is also a lack of communication via imaginative or imitative play.

3. *Narrow and/or repetitive range of interests or behaviors.* The autistic person has an inappropriately intense fascination with a particular subject, or may be overly preoccupied with the parts of an object. Typically, the child is inflexible and has ritualistic behaviors, including repetitive body movements such as rocking or arm flapping.

*Other qualifying criteria include* early onset (before three years old) of problems in at least one of the areas of: pretend/imaginary play, social interactions, or the pragmatic use of language.

## ASPERGER'S SYNDROME

Symptoms of Asperger's include:

- impaired ability to utilize social cues such as body language or tone of voice
- impaired ability to understand irony or other "subtext" of communication
- "concrete" thinking
- restricted eye contact and socialization
- appearance as distant or a loner
- limited range of encyclopedic interests
- didactic, verbose, monotone, droning voice
- perseverative, odd behaviors
- over-sensitivity to certain stimuli
- unusual movements.

The official DSM-IV criteria for Asperger's (APA 1994) are similar to those for autistic disorder, except do not include the "communication" problem areas above. In other words, Asperger's people are autistic people who talk well. Although verbal speech is preserved in Asperger's, other communication problems certainly exist.

You can hear a soudtrack of two children with Asperger's at the author's website at www.pediatricneurology.com/aspergers_sound.htm. Once you hear their typical droning voice, you'll never forget it.

Asperger's syndrome is discussed in greater detail in the following chapter.

## PDD-NOS (PDD-NOT OTHERWISE SPECIFIED)

The diagnosis of PDD-NOS is invoked for children in the autistic spectrum who do not completely fit into one of the other categories.

## RETT'S SYNDROME

This is a neurodegenerative disorder of girls who have normal initial development, but then show marked loss of developmental milestones and social interactions, slowing of head growth, and wringing hand movements.

### CHILDHOOD DISINTEGRATIVE DISORDER

Children with this disorder develop normally for at least the first two years, and then have a deterioration sufficient to meet criteria for autistic disorder; but also have show deterioration of language, muscle control, social, play, and toilet training skills. These children need to be carefully evaluated for an underlying neurodegenerative process.

## Expanded autistic spectrum disorders

Next, we turn our attention to those autistic spectrum disorders that are not included in DSM-IV.

### HIGH-FUNCTIONING AUTISM

For some authors, this term is synonymous with Asperger's syndrome. For others, it implies milder autism without retardation, or PDD-NOS. Given the lack of consensus for the meaning of this term, it is probably best not to use it.

### NON-VERBAL LEARNING DISABILITIES

Non-verbal learning disabilities (NVLDs) are a cluster of symptoms presumably related to poor ability to integrate information. These children have trouble with the ability to integrate it all together, i.e., to see the big gestalt picture rather than the details. In short, they "can't see the forest for the trees." These tasks are usually carried out by the brain's non-dominant hemisphere (typically the right hemisphere). Even though rote verbal language is spared, non-verbal areas of difficulty may be debilitating.

Although verbal communication is highly prized in school (good talkers, readers, and writers), up to two thirds of communication actually occurs non-verbally (Thompson 1996). Thus, in the long run, the maladaptive learning of NVLD may be more destructive than typical LD. Estimates are that 0.1 to 1% of the population has an NVLD, compared with perhaps as much as 10% of the population with an LD (Thompson

1996), although these numbers may be an artifact of who and how we test.

Difficulty integrating non-verbal information occurs in three main areas:

□ *Motor skills:*

- *Gross motor*—clumsy, unbalanced walking leading to clinging behaviors, bumping into things, fear of climbing, hesitant to explore physically, difficulty bike-riding, and uncoordinated at sports.

- *Fine motor*—difficulty using scissors, shoe tying (which she'll talk herself through), and poor handwriting using awkward and tight grip.

□ *Visual/spatial orientation skills*, with an inability to form visual images:

- Resultant focus on detail rather than the important gestalt.

- Labels everything verbally, since that is the only—albeit not always accurate—way she can process the visual/spatial information. For example, she may find her way home by counting houses and labeling landmarks verbally.

- The elaborate "naming" strategies break down with changes in routine, leading to an inability to cope with change.

- Unaware where she is in space, unaware of where to place answers on the homework sheet, or how to navigate the school.

□ *Social/communication skills:*

- Trouble integrating non-verbal communication with verbal communication in order to achieve full social interaction.

- Clearly appears to want social acceptance (vs. Asperger's, where the children usually do not appear interested socially).

- Very literal interpretation of others; concrete thinking; seeing the world in black and white; trouble understanding dishonesty; trouble seeing hidden meanings, prompting others to say "You know what I meant!"—when they didn't.

- Don't read the social cues of give-and-take conversation, thus appearing self-centered, weird, or impolite.

- Typically labeled as "annoying" because of their dependence on others, their constant speech, and their misinterpretation of social cues.

NVLD symptoms change through the lifespan.

□ *Toddlers*:

- Uncoordinated (gross motor and fine motor).

- Trouble with social interactions, non-verbal cues (such as a peer's facial expression of "Enough is enough!"), and adjustments to change. They may appear "confused."

- Warning signal: You always have to tell the child, "I shouldn't have to tell you that." Obviously, with these kids, you *do* have to tell them. That's how you know there is a problem.

- Trouble with spatial orientation.

□ *Young children*:

- Often exceptional rote speech, memory, and reading skill, which the children use to compensate for lack of intuitive social interaction. The child tries to "remember" how to interact, rather than the skill coming automatically in each different situation.

- The pedantic speech patterns and the exceptional reading abilities may be interpreted as preciousness.

- Clumsy monologues replace typical give-and-take conversations.

□ *Older children*:

- Academic problems in the later elementary years with organization, inferential reading, and written output.

- Math facts better than concepts.

- Typically Performance IQ<Verbal IQ.

- Sustains focus on details, does not attend to big picture.

- A life of social blunders, without ever figuring out why.

- May have secondary depression or anxiety.

NVLD is determined by neuropsychological testing, whereas Asperger's is determined by detailed history and observation. There is great overlap in these two conditions—perhaps due to comorbidity; or perhaps, as some authors feel, they are essentially the same condition but labeled by different specialties. However, people with Asperger's are primarily notable for *not appearing* interested in forming human bonds. (The degree to which Asperger's kids actually are painfully aware of their trouble making bonds is debated in the literature. Nevertheless, they typically appear uninterested.) NVLD kids, though, do typically appear interested in human bonds—even though they may be clueless how to actually achieve them successfully. Additionally, children with Asperger's typically have more diminished "symbolic play" than in NVLD.

So, how about this for a gross oversimplification? NVLD kids recognize that you exist while they miss the subtext of what you are saying. Asperger's kids appear as if outside a window as they miss the subtext of what you are saying.

## SEMANTIC-PRAGMATIC LANGUAGE DISORDER

"Semantics" refers to the ability to use and understand words, phrases, and sentences, including abstract concepts and idioms. "Pragmatics" refers to the practical ability to use language in a social setting, such as knowing what is appropriate to say, where and when to say it, the give and take nature of a conversation, and the ability to know what the other person does or does not already know. Thus, semantic-pragmatic language disorder (SPLD) kids have:

- difficulty understanding the literal meaning of words and sentences (semantics)

- difficulty with abstract words, words about emotions, idioms, and words about status such as "expert" (semantics)

- difficulty extracting the central idea (pragmatics)

- trouble with the appropriate rules of conversation, such as talking "at" you or using monologues (pragmatics).

This inability to understand verbal language and the purpose of language leads to the typical secondary problems we have discussed above.

Here is what we might expect in the life of a child with SPLD through the years:

- often very easy infants

- delayed development of speech with few words even by two years old

- trouble with creative or symbolic play

- simple speech improves with therapy, but in school child is "odd"

- good rote skills in math and computers, perhaps, but poor writing and socialization skills

- parrot back more than they understand, leading to an aura of intellectual maturity out of synch with their social skills

- trouble understanding what others are really thinking or feeling, i.e. trouble with theory of mind

- many have fine motor problems; some have gross motor difficulties as well

- they may have trouble knowing what is socially acceptable, but are not usually conduct disorder teens

- may be "eccentric" adults.

SPLD can be differentiated from Asperger's as follows:

- SPLD kids tend to have more early speech delays than Asperger's.

- SPLD kids tend to have somewhat better socialization skills than Asperger's.

- The appropriate label may change over time as the child matures.

## HYPERLEXIA

Hyperlexia is a condition, occurring almost always in boys, where autistic spectrum symptoms are accompanied by a striking capacity for rote reading. By 18–24 months of age, these kids have taught themselves the ability to name letters and numbers. By three years old, they may read printed words, exceeding even their ability to talk. By five years old, all have a fascination with the printed word. Some of the children seemed to have a mild regression at 18–24 months (less severe than as in autism).

In addition to this unusual reading skill, there are the other typical common autistic spectrum disorder symptoms we have seen, such as:

□ *language problems*:

- good rote or echoed language
- trouble translating words into larger gestalt ideas
- repetitive, idiosyncratic speech
- pragmatic language problems
- unusual prosody (rhythm) of speech.

□ *socialization problems*:

- see "Secondary problems resulting from failure to understand" (p.90)
- stereotyped, ritualistic behaviors
- anxiety
- trouble making friends.

The above description is based on an article by Phyllis Kupperman and others from the Center for Speech and Language Disorders (Kupperman *et al.* n.d.).

## ADHD?

ADHDers typically have adequate capacity for empathy—but may have trouble inhibiting their behavior long enough to *show* it. Conversely, many children on the autistic spectrum may appear to have a short attention span, but this may actually be due to an inability to stay focused on situations they don't understand. Of course, ADHD and ASD can—and do—frequently co-occur as parts of the syndrome mix.

It is probably best to consider ADHD not as part of, but as sometimes sharing the following symptoms with autistic spectrum disorders:

☐ *Poor reading of social cues*—"Johnny, you're such a social klutz. Can't you see that the other children think that's weird?"

☐ *Poor ability to utilize "self-talk" to work through a problem*—"Johnny, what were you thinking?! Did you ever think this through?"

☐ *Poor sense of self-awareness*—Johnny's true answer to the above question is probably: "I don't have a clue. I guess I wasn't actually thinking."

☐ *Better performance with predictable routine.*

☐ *Poor generalization of rules*—"Johnny, I told you to shake hands with your teachers. Why didn't you shake hands with the *principal?*".

## Conclusion (finally!)

The classification of the autistic spectrum disorders is in a state of flux. The problems can overlap, cause each other, occur simultaneously in different combinations and severities, change over time, and don't even have one "official" group attempting the classification of the whole spectrum.

However, unless we know all of the possible syndromes, we will continue to squeeze everyone into the same category or two. Most importantly, unless we know the full range of the autistic spectrum disorders, we will not identify all of the individual symptoms that require treatment.

With trepidation, I offer the following gross oversimplifications. I am reminded of my professor's comment on the first day of medical school: "One third of what I am going to tell you this year is wrong. Unfortunately, I don't know which third."

- Autistic spectrum disorders are marked by difficulty in communication/socialization in areas other than the literal meaning of words.

- Once a child has trouble with getting the big picture of communication and socialization, there will often be secondary symptoms, such as anxiety, holding back from peers, a rigid adherence to sameness, a relative preference for things (which are predictable) rather than people, and an appearance of "oddness."

- Asperger's and autism share primarily the difficulty of recognizing the existence of others—trouble with theory of mind. People with Asperger's can talk; autism usually has limited speech.

- Asperger's children *appear* less interested in forming bonds and have more trouble with "theory of mind" than NVLD and semantic-pragmatic disorder.

- NVLDs are marked by integration problems of pragmatic language gestalt; spatial orientation; and motor coordination.

- Hyperlexia is marked by fascination with the printed word starting at an early age.

- "High-functioning autism" is used by different authors to mean either autistic disorder with relatively spared speech and cognition, Asperger's syndrome, or PDD-NOS.

Autistic spectrum disorders such as Asperger's tend to be highly "comorbid"—occur in conjunction with other conditions of the syndrome mix. ADHD, anxiety, obsessive-compulsive disorder (OCD), and sensory integration problems are particularly common.

Table 5.1 The major communication disorders (oversimplified)

| Problem areas | Traditional learning/language disabilities | Hyperlexia | Semantic–pragmatic language disorder (SPCD) | Non-verbal learning disabilities (NVLD) | Asperger's syndrome | Autistic disorder |
|---|---|---|---|---|---|---|
| Semantic problems (literal verbal/written language) | ++++ | 0 | +++ | 0 | 0 | ++++ |
| Delays in early verbal language | +++ | 0 or ++ | +++ | 0 | 0 | ++++ |
| Pragmatic language ("What's the real purpose of this conversation?") | 0 | +++ | +++ | +++ | ++++ | ++++ |
| Theory of mind/Relatedness/Empathy | 0 | + | + | + | ++++ | ++++ |
| Eye contact problems | 0 | + | + | + | ++++ | ++++ |
| Restricted/stereotyped range of interests | 0 | ++ | ++ | ++ | +++ | ++++ |
| Appears uninterested in making friends | 0 | + | + | + | ++++ | ++++ |
| Pretend or symbolic play problems | 0 | + | + | + | ++++ | ++++ |
| Spatial problems | 0 (+++ in perceptual learning disabilities) | Varies | + | ++++ | + | Varies |
| Fascination with written words | 0 | ++++ | 0 | 0 | 0 | 0 |
| Gross and fine motor problems | 0 | Varies | 0 | ++++ | + | + |

Key: 0 Not a significant problem area; + Typically a minor problem area; ++ Typically a significant problem area; +++ Typically a major problem area; ++++ Typically a severe problem area

## Chapter 6

# Asperger's Syndrome and Its Treatment

Tony Attwood

> The brain is wired differently, not defectively. The child prioritizes the pursuit of knowledge, perfection, truth, and the understanding of the physical world above feelings and interpersonal experiences. This can lead to valued talents, but also to vulnerabilities in the social world.

For an introduction to Asperger's syndrome, see the overview chapter on autistic spectrum disorders.

## Adjustment to being different

By definition, a child with a developmental disorder such as Asperger's syndrome is different from other children. Eventually, parents and professionals are able to identify the diagnostic term that describes the unusual profile of abilities. However, the child with Asperger's syndrome will have also recognized that he or she is different from other children. Some children with Asperger's syndrome will internalize their emotional reaction to being different, while others externalize their emotional reaction.

## Internalizing thoughts and feelings
### DEPRESSION

Children with Asperger's syndrome do not know intuitively how to play or interact with their peers, and can be subject to ridicule, teasing and exclusion—leading to damaged self-esteem. Social competence and friendship abilities are highly valued by typical children, and not being successful in these abilities can lead some children with Asperger's syndrome to internalize their thoughts and feelings with self-criticism, and increased social withdrawal. Such children, sometimes as young as six years, may then develop a reactive depression as a result of insight into being different.

### IMAGINATION

A more constructive internalization of thoughts and feelings can be to escape into imagination. The child develops a vivid and complex imaginary world, sometimes with imaginary friends. In this fantasy world, the child is successful socially and academically. Sometimes the degree of imaginative thought can lead to an avid interest in reading and writing fiction. The escape into imagination can be a psychologically constructive adaptation, but there are risks during adolescence, when this retreat into a fantasy world may lead to the exclusion of other activities, and to other people misinterpreting the adolescent's intentions or state of mind.

## Externalizing thoughts and feelings
### ANGER AND ARROGANCE

An alternative to internalizing negative thoughts and feelings about being different is to externalize them. "It is not my fault but your fault." The child may over-compensate for the lack of competence in social situations by completely denying any problems and developing a sense of arrogance and anger towards others. Suggestions from remedial programs or therapy are vehemently rejected. The child can also become arrogant, which may lead to conduct problems. Unfortunately, one of the consequences of arrogance, denial, and the immaturity of empathy associated with Asperger's syndrome, is to seek resolution and retribution for social embarrassment by physical retaliation.

## IMITATION

A more psychologically constructive way of externalizing thoughts and feelings is to observe and imitate the characteristics of those peers who are socially successful. The child learns how to "act" in social situations by becoming another child. Some children with Asperger's syndrome can be remarkably astute in their observation abilities, copying gestures, tone of voice and mannerisms. This can be a constructive way of achieving social inclusion if the child mimics an appropriate role model. Unfortunately, some adolescents with Asperger's syndrome may imitate the socially popular but notorious bad guys at school.

## Should you explain the diagnosis to the child?

The answer is a resounding "yes." Clinical experience indicates that explaining the diagnosis to the child with Asperger's syndrome is extremely important. This will help prevent the development of inappropriate compensatory mechanisms, and encourage the child to accept treatment programs.

### THE ATTRIBUTES ACTIVITY

In the Attributes Activity that I have developed, a listing of the child's "Qualities" and "Difficulties" helps to explain the diagnosis to the child and their family. The clinician gathers family members, including the person who has recently been diagnosed as having Asperger's syndrome. First, large sheets of paper are attached to the wall, or a large whiteboard with colored pens can be used. Each sheet is divided into two columns: "Qualities" and "Difficulties." I always suggest that another family member is the first person to do the activity, which is to identify his or her own personal qualities and difficulties. These can include practical abilities, knowledge, personality, and the expression and management of feelings. After the initial focus person has made some suggestions, which the clinician writes on the paper/board, the family members add their own suggestions. The clinician ensures that this is a positive activity, commenting on the various attributes and ensuring there are more qualities than difficulties. The child with Asperger's syndrome is then able to observe and participate in the activity, and understand what is expected when it is his or her turn.

The clinician comments on each quality and difficulty nominated by the child with Asperger's syndrome and then explains that scientists are often looking for patterns. When they find a consistent pattern, they like to give it a name. Reference is then made to Dr. Hans Asperger who, over 60 years ago, saw at his clinic in Vienna many children with similar characteristics. He published the first clinical description that has become known as Asperger's syndrome.

The clinician usually says to the child, "Congratulations, you have Asperger's syndrome," and explains that this means they are not mad, bad or defective, but have a *different* way of thinking. The discussion continues with an explanation of how some of the child's talents or qualities are due to having Asperger's syndrome, such as impressing people with his or her knowledge about the Titanic, ability to draw with photographic realism, attention to detail and being naturally talented in mathematics. This is to introduce the benefits of having the characteristics of Asperger's syndrome.

The next stage is to discuss the difficulties and the strategies needed to improve specific abilities at home and at school. This can include the advantages of guidance and counseling in social understanding, cognitive behavior therapy or medication that is used to help with emotion management, and ideas to help with making friends. The clinician provides a summary of the person's qualities and difficulties that are due to having Asperger's syndrome and mentions successful people in the areas of science, information technology, politics, and the arts who benefited from the signs of Asperger's syndrome in their own profile of abilities—such as Einstein, Thomas Jefferson and Mozart.

The activity closes with explanation of some of my personal thoughts on Asperger's syndrome. Such individuals have different priorities, perception of the world, and way of thinking. The brain is wired differently not defectively. The person prioritizes the pursuit of knowledge, perfection, truth, and the understanding of the physical world above feelings and interpersonal experiences. This can lead to valued talents, but also vulnerabilities in the social world.

## Making friends: motivations and encouragement
### Five stages of making friends

Having observed the social development of well over a thousand children and adults with Asperger's syndrome, I have identified five stages in the motivation and experience of friendships and relationships.

- An interest in the physical world.
- Wanting to play with friends.
- Making friends.
- Searching for a partner.
- Maintaining the partnership.

#### AN INTEREST IN THE PHYSICAL WORLD

Very young children with Asperger's syndrome may not be interested in the activities of their peers. They are usually more interested in understanding the physical world than the social world, and may enter the pre-school playground to explore the drainage system of the school or to search for insects and reptiles. The social activities of their peers are perceived as boring with incomprehensible social rules. The child is content with solitude.

#### WANTING TO PLAY WITH FRIENDS

In the early school years, children with Asperger's syndrome recognize that other children are having fun socializing, and want to be included in the social activities. However, despite their intellectual ability, their level of social maturity is usually at least two years behind their peers, and they may have special difficulties with reciprocal and cooperative play. The child with Asperger's syndrome may long for social inclusion, social success and a friend. This can be when the child becomes acutely aware of being different to his or her peers and the adjustment strategies described above may begin.

#### MAKING FRIENDS

In the middle school years, the child may make genuine friendships. Friendships with typical children may be brief, with a tendency for the child with Asperger's syndrome to be too dominant or to have too rigid a view of friendship. Some typical children who are naturally kind, understanding and "maternal" can be tolerant and become genuine friends. Sometimes the friendship is with similar, socially isolated children who share the same interests.

### SEARCHING FOR A PARTNER

In late adolescence, teenagers with Asperger's syndrome may seek more than a platonic friendship with like-minded individuals and express a longing for a partner. They can be confused by the new dimensions to adolescent friendships and especially aspects of self-disclosure and sexuality. Adolescents with Asperger's syndrome often become more acutely aware that they are different to their peers and need a partner rather than a friend. The partner they seek is someone who understands them and provides emotional support and guidance in the social world—someone to "mother" them.

### MAINTAINING THE PARTNERSHIP

Eventually, perhaps when emotionally and socially more mature, the adult with Asperger's syndrome may find a lifetime partner. However, both partners probably need relationship counseling to facilitate the adjustments needed in an unconventional relationship. We now have literature and relationship counseling programs for couples where one partner has Asperger's syndrome.

We are only just beginning to design therapy programs to encourage friendship skills. Parents may provide some guidance at home, but schools will need to be aware that they must develop a social curriculum for a child with Asperger's syndrome with an emphasis on friendship skills, and provide appropriate staff training and resources. The following treatment suggestions are designed for each of the developmental stages of friendship that occur in typical children.

## Ages 3 to 6 years

### AN ADULT ACTING AS A FRIEND

Very young children with Asperger's syndrome may prefer to interact and play with adults more than with peers. It is important that adults, especially parents, observe the natural play of the child's peers—noting the games, equipment, rules, and language. They can then practice the same play with the child but with an adult "acting" as his or her same-age friend. This includes using "child speak"; namely, the speech of children rather than adults. It is important that the adult role-plays examples of being a good friend, and also role-plays unfriendly acts, such as disagreements and teasing. Appropriate and inappropriate responses can be enacted to provide the child with a range of responses. Once the child has rehearsed with an adult, who can easily modify the pace of play and amount of instruction, he or she can practice social play with another child. Perhaps, an older sibling can act as a friend, and provide further practice before the skills are used openly with the peer group.

In the early childhood years, a good friend is someone who shares, takes turns and helps. It is important that when an adult is playing with the child, the activities involve an equivalent level of abilities and contribution in the choice of activity. Activities can be undertaken in a cooperative rather than competitive way. Turn taking should be a key feature of interactive play. For example, practice taking turns in finding and connecting each piece of a jigsaw puzzle. To encourage assistance, the adult can feign difficulty and ask the child for help, commenting that good friends help each other.

### SOCIAL DOCUMENTARIES

Use a video camera to make short and interesting videos of the child's everyday social experiences. For example, film the child playing with his or her peers in the sandpit, or involved in social games such as chasing, or hide-and-seek. The pause and replay buttons can be used to focus on particular cues and responses. Young children with Asperger's syndrome often enjoy watching videos and television. This activity can be used to improve friendship skills.

## Ages 6 to 9 years

At this stage, typical children start to recognize that they need a friend to play certain games, and that that friend must like those games. They become more aware of the thoughts and feelings of their peers and how their actions and comments can hurt both physically and emotionally. Most children are prepared sometimes to inhibit their intentions and to accept and incorporate the influences, preferences, and goals of their friends in their play. There is less of a dominant/submissive quality. Rather, helping—especially mutual help—is one of the indices of friendship at this stage. Around the age of eight years, typical children develop the concept of a best friend as not only their first choice for social play, but also as someone who helps in practical terms. She knows how to fix the computer, and in times of emotional stress, he cheers me up when I'm feeling sad.

### SOCIAL STORIES™

Teacher and expert on children with autistic spectrum disorders, Carol Gray, has developed the strategy of Social Stories™, which are remarkably effective in enabling the child to understand the cues and responses for specific social situations. The guidance is not only in what to do, but more importantly, why there are certain codes of social conduct and expectations. Children with Asperger's syndrome will need this type of practical guidance in relating to their peers in the playground and the classroom. A Social Story is written as a collaborative exercise between the adult and child, and the story is consistent with the child's reading ability. The Social Story describes a situation, skill, or concept in terms of relevant social cues, perspectives and common responses. The goal is to share accurate social and emotional information in a reassuring and informative manner that is easily understood by the child with Asperger's syndrome. The first Social Story and at least 50% of subsequent Social Stories should describe, affirm and consolidate existing abilities and knowledge and what the child does well. This can avoid the problem of a Social Story being only associated with failure. Social Stories can also be written as a means of recording achievements in the use of new knowledge and strategies. Preparing Social Stories also enables others to understand the perspective of the child, and why his or her social behavior can appear unduly confused, anxious, aggressive, or disobedient.

Social Stories use positive language and a constructive approach. The suggestions are what to do rather than what not to do. The text will include *descriptive sentences* that provide factual information or statements; but one of the reasons for the success of Social Stories is the use of *perspective sentences*. These sentences are written to explain a person's perception of the physical and mental world. Perspective sentences describe thoughts, emotions, beliefs, opinions, motivation, and knowledge. They are specifically included to improve theory of mind abilities (see p.87). Carol Gray recommends including *cooperative sentences* to identify who can be of assistance, which can be a very important aspect of emotion management; and *directive sentences*, that suggest a response or choice of responses in a particular situation. *Affirmative sentences* explain a commonly shared value, opinion or rule—the reason why specific codes of conduct have been established and why there is the expectation of conformity. *Control sentences* are written by the child to identify personal strategies to help remember what to do. The Social Story will also need a title, which should reflect its essential characteristics or criteria. Carol Gray has developed a Social Story formula such that the text describes more than directs. (See the Further Reading section for a useful video on this topic.)

While a Social Story provides the rationale and script of what to do, there will need to be opportunities to rehearse and practice new social understanding in real-life situations. Teachers and parents may rehearse aspects of social play with selected children who understand the difficulties of the child with Asperger's syndrome—a "dress rehearsal."

## Ages 9 to 13 years

In the third stage of friendship, a friend is chosen because of special attributes in their abilities and personality. A friend is someone who genuinely cares with complimentary attitudes, ideas, and values. There is a strong need to be liked by one's peers and a mutual sharing of experiences and thoughts. With such self-disclosure, there is the recognition of being trustworthy and seeking advice not only for practical problems but also for interpersonal issues. There is a need for companionship and greater selectivity and durability in the friendship alliances. At this stage, there is a distinct gender split and peer pressure becomes increasingly important. Peer group acceptance and values become more important than the opinion of parents. Friends also support each other in terms of managing emotions. If the child is sad, close friends can provide the necessary reassurance and optimism; if angry, they can provide the calm required to prevent him or her getting into trouble.

### SOCIAL ENGINEERING

As the peer group becomes more important in establishing self-esteem, teachers and parents will need to undertake some "social engineering" with regard to how they group the children. Parents can identify a prospective friend and arrange a family outing or activity at home that includes the potential friend, with some careful monitoring and guidance to encourage an enjoyable time for both parties. They may need to encourage the peer group to consider the perspective of the child with Asperger's syndrome.

### ENCOURAGING A BUDDY

Individual children who have a natural rapport with a child with Asperger's syndrome can be guided and encouraged to be a mentor in the classroom, playground, and in social situations. Their advice may be accepted as having greater value than that of parents or teachers. It is also important to encourage friends or peers to help children with Asperger's syndrome regulate their moods. Peers can step in and help them calm down if they are becoming agitated or tormented. Friends may need to provide reassurance if such children are anxious, and to cheer them up when sad. Children with Asperger's syndrome will also need advice and encouragement to give back reciprocal emotional support. They will need to be taught how to recognize the signs of distress or agitation in their friends, and how to respond. Social Stories can be used for this age group, with the topics being aspects of friendship such as giving compliments, emotional support, and being a good listener.

### TEAMWORK SKILLS

At this stage, the existing remedial programs use strategies to develop teamwork rather than friendship skills. Attending a program on teamwork skills for sports or employment may be considered more acceptable to young teenagers with Asperger's syndrome, who may be sensitive to any suggestion that they need remedial programs to have friends.

### DRAMA CLASSES

Another strategy to help the adolescent who is sensitive to being publicly identified as having few friends is to adapt speech and drama classes. This is an appropriate and effective strategy especially for young teenagers. Those with Asperger's syndrome can learn and practice conversational scripts, self-disclosure, body language, facial expression, and tone of voice for particular situations, and role-play people they know who are socially successful.

## Ages 13 to 18 years

In the previous developmental stage of friendship there may be a small core of close friends; but in this stage, the breadth and depth of friendship increases. There can be different friends for different needs, such as comfort, humor, or practical advice. A friend is defined as someone who "accepts me for who I am" or "thinks the same way about things." A friend provides a sense of personal identity and is compatible with one's own personality.

### SELF-HELP GUIDES

There are multiple sources of guidance. We now have several books, such as *Freaks, Geeks and Asperger's Syndrome* by Luke Jackson (see Further Reading section), that have been written by teenagers with Asperger's syndrome as self-help guides for fellow teenagers with Asperger's syndrome. Parent support groups have also established regular meetings for adolescents with Asperger's syndrome to enable discussion of issues such as friendships, sexuality and high school. A team of parents usually coordinates the groups with advice from professionals who are often invited to the meetings and facilitate discussion and suggestions.

### THE INTERNET

The Internet has become the modern equivalent of the dance hall in terms of an opportunity for young people to meet. The great advantage of this form of communication to the person with Asperger's syndrome is that they often have a greater eloquence in disclosing and expressing their inner self and feelings through typing rather than conversation. However, parents will need to carefully supervise Internet friendships as teenagers with Asperger's syndrome are vulnerable to abuse from someone who appears to have friendly intentions.

## Therapy suggestions for all stages in friendship
### POSITIVE FEEDBACK

Children with Asperger's syndrome need more positive feedback. If completing a mathematics activity, children know they have the correct solution by confirming the answer on a calculator. When completing a jigsaw puzzle, they know they have been successful when all the pieces fit together and complete the picture. But how does one know when he was "correct" in socializing? It is essential that adults and peers recognize, and comment on, what the child with Asperger's syndrome did in an interaction that was socially appropriate. Otherwise, the only feedback is criticism when he or she has made a social error.

### BOOKS ON FRIENDSHIP

There are storybooks, novels, and guides written for typical children of various ages that describe and explore aspects of friendship. These books can be read to the child with Asperger's syndrome by parents, or chosen as class reading material and be the basis of class discussions.

### THE ART OF CONVERSATION

Speech pathologists can provide individual and group activities to encourage the pragmatic aspects of language. Throughout the stages of friendship, the child will need guidance in the pragmatic aspects—the "art of conversation."

PROGRAMS TO AVOID BEING TEASED AND BULLIED

The school may need to implement an anti-bullying program that can be modified for children with Asperger's syndrome. While we hope that social inclusion is a positive experience, inevitably the child with Asperger's syndrome will be the target for teasing, bullying, and deliberate exclusion. We now have several programs to reduce the frequency and different types of bullying and teasing designed specifically for children with Asperger's syndrome.

## Managing emotions
### Cognitive behavior therapy

Research studies, clinical experience, and autobiographies have confirmed that children with Asperger's syndrome have considerable difficulty with the understanding and expression of emotions, and are at risk of developing an anxiety disorder, depression, or problems with anger management. However, we are only just beginning to learn how to modify effective psychological treatments such as cognitive behavior therapy (CBT) for children with Asperger's syndrome. CBT has been developed and refined over several decades and, using rigorous scientific evaluations, proven to be effective in changing the way a person thinks about and responds to feelings such as anxiety, sadness, and anger.

CBT focuses on aspects of direct applicability to children with Asperger's syndrome, who are known to have deficits and distortions in thinking about thoughts and feelings, especially determining whether an act was deliberate or accidental, and a tendency to make a literal interpretation of what someone says or does.

Cognitive behavior therapy programs for children with Asperger's syndrome have two stages. The first stage is *affective education*, where the child learns about emotions. This stage of therapy includes working on the connection between thoughts, feelings, and behavior. The child learns how he may conceptualize emotions and perceive various situations.

The subsequent stage is *cognitive restructuring*, and includes a schedule of activities to practice new cognitive skills.

## The Emotional Toolbox

This writer (Tony Attwood) has developed the concept of an Emotional Toolbox, a successful strategy for "cognitive restructuring"—one of the main activities used to help repair a specific feeling.

From an early age, children understand that a toolbox contains a variety of different tools to repair a machine or fix a household problem. The therapist works with the child to identify different types of "tools" to fix the problems associated with negative emotions, especially anxiety, sadness, and anger. The range of tools can be divided into those that:

- quickly and constructively release emotional energy
- slowly reduce emotional energy
- improve thinking.

### PHYSICAL TOOLS

A hammer can represent tools or actions that physically release emotional energy. A picture of a hammer is drawn on a large sheet of paper and the child suggests safe and appropriate physical activities. For young children this may include going for a run, bouncing on the trampoline, or going on a swing. For older children, sports practice and dancing may be used to "let off steam" or release emotional energy.

### RELAXATION TOOLS

Relaxation tools help to calm the person and lower the heart rate. A paint-brush could be used to illustrate this category of tools, and activities could include drawing, reading, and listening to music. Children with Asperger's syndrome often find that solitude is their most relaxing activity. They may need to retreat to a quiet, secluded sanctuary as an effective emotional repair mechanism. Young children may relax by using gentle rocking actions and engaging in a repetitive action. This can include manipulating an object such as a stress ball that has the same soothing qualities as an adult manipulating worry beads.

### SOCIAL TOOLS

This group of tools uses other people as a means of managing feelings. The goal is to find and be with someone (or an animal or pet) that can help change the mood. The social activity will need to be enjoyable and without the stress that can sometimes be associated with social interaction, especially when interacting with more than one other person. Remember the description, "two's company, three's a crowd."

## THINKING TOOLS

The child can nominate another type of implement, such as a wrench, to represent a category of tools that can be used to change thinking, improve knowledge, or challenge inappropriate beliefs. The child is encouraged to use his or her intellectual strength to control feelings using a variety of techniques. Self-talk can be used, such as "I can control my feelings" or "I can stay calm" when under stress. The words are reassuring and encourage self-confidence and self-esteem.

## SPECIAL INTEREST TOOLS

Children with Asperger's syndrome can experience intense pleasure when engaged in their special interest. The degree of enjoyment may be far in excess of other potentially pleasurable experiences. The child can be encouraged to engage in his or her interest as a means of restoring the emotional equilibrium—a counterbalance of pleasure. The activity can sometimes appear to be mesmerizing and dominating all thought, but this can be effective at excluding negative thoughts such as anxiety and anger. When the child with Asperger's syndrome is very distressed, the most effective emotional restoratives are solitude and becoming totally absorbed in the special interest.

## MEDICATION

Medication is sometimes prescribed for children with Asperger's syndrome to manage emotions. If the child is showing clear signs of a diagnosable anxiety disorder or a clinical depression (which may be expressed as episodes of intense anger, irritability, or apathy), then medication may be recommended. It is important to ensure that medication is not the only tool we add to the Emotional Toolbox.

## Learning: abilities and styles

### Profile of learning abilities

Children with Asperger's syndrome have an unusual and uneven profile of learning skills, and a learning style that can be confusing to teachers. Some children with Asperger's syndrome can be quite talented in terms of reading, mathematical, and mechanical abilities. While the child's average intelligence test score or overall IQ (intelligence quotient) may be within the normal range or even superior range, some individual test scores in the profile may be within the mildly retarded range.

Research has indicated there may be a tendency for children with Asperger's syndrome to have a higher verbal than visual reasoning IQ. However, the same research has indicated that some children with the diagnostic characteristics of Asperger's syndrome have the reverse pattern—a higher visual than verbal IQ. The general consensus among academics and clinicians is that the examination of the profile of learning or cognitive skills should not be used to confirm a diagnosis but will provide invaluable information with regard to the learning profile and learning style.

### Learning style

#### VERBALIZERS AND VISUALIZERS

If the child has a relatively higher verbal IQ, his or her learning style may be described as being a "*verbalizer*," and the child may succeed academically by reading about the subject rather than participating in the classroom activities. If the child is a "*visualizer*," then learning may be facilitated by silent demonstrations, films, and diagrams, and the advice that "a picture is worth a thousand words." Such children can be natural engineers. However, the child may have in his or her mind the "picture" or solution to a problem, but not the thousand words, to provide an explanation. Such children can have difficulty converting thoughts into speech. For both groups, remedial programs may be more successful if the curriculum or concept is explained on a computer screen rather than in the social and linguistic context of the classroom.

## FEAR OF MAKING A MISTAKE

There can be a pathological fear of making a mistake or failure, and some activities may be refused if there is the possibility of not being perfect. This fear may be more powerful than the good that could come to a child who can be very attentive to details. Social Stories (Gray and White 2002) can be used to explain the importance of learning more from errors than success, and that the child is not stupid for making a mistake. Children with Asperger's syndrome can be very sensitive about appearing stupid.

## ENCOURAGING MOTIVATION

A useful motivational tool is to appeal to the child's intellectual vanity, replacing personal delight with unemotional comments that the work indicates how smart they are. The usual motivation of praise from the teacher may not be as effective as with other children. This approach may help overcome a common problem: the motivation of the child with Asperger's syndrome.

## ADAPTATIONS TO EXAMINATIONS AND TESTS

The child may need extra time, supervision, and the facility to type rather than write answers and essays. Otherwise, the child with Asperger's syndrome may lose marks on timed tests because of difficulties due to problems working quickly, being pedantic, being distracted by details, and by handwriting problems.

The teacher or parent may have to act as an "executive secretary" with guidance and allowances for problems with executive skills. Without this help, there may also be problems with executive function skills (see p.43), especially organizational and planning skills that affect school projects, and homework.

## A ONE-TRACK MIND

The child may prefer to follow his or her own idiosyncratic ideas rather than copying the other children, or heeding the advice of the teacher, and may be very rigid in thinking—a "one-track mind." There can be difficulties switching tracks when a strategy or solution is not successful, and problems losing the train of thought when interrupted. Teachers will need to explain that there are many ways to solve some problems, and that the smart thing to do is try another way or ask for help.

## Special interests

Special interests can develop in young children with Asperger's syndrome as early as age two to three years, and may commence with a preoccupation with parts of objects. The interest can be spinning the wheels of toy cars or manipulating electrical switches.

The next, or first, stage for some children is a fascination with a specific category of objects and the accumulation of as many examples as possible. Sometimes the collections comprise items typically acquired by other children, such as unusual stones, but some can be quite eccentric, such as drain covers.

The child's play can also be somewhat eccentric in that he or she can pretend to be the special interest. One child had a special interest in toilets and in the playground pretended to be a blocked toilet. Another child, attending a special "costume day" at school (where children typically chose film characters or animals) went as a washing machine—his special interest.

The next stage is for children to acquire information regarding a topic or concept. Common topics or concepts are transportion, animals, and electronics. Some of the interests are developmentally appropriate and typical of their peers, such as Thomas the Tank Engine, dinosaurs, castles, and computer games; while other interests can be unusual, such as vacuum cleaners and alarm systems. The reason for the interest is usually idiosyncratic, and not necessarily because the topic is popular with peers or is the "currency" between friends.

The focus of the interest invariably changes, but at a time dictated by the child, and is replaced by another special interest that is the choice of the child, not a parent or teacher. The complexity and number of interests varies according to the child's developmental level and intellectual capacity. Over time there is a progression to multiple and more abstract or complex interests, such as periods of history or specific countries/cultures.

## The special interests of girls

Clinical experience suggests that boys and girls with Asperger's syndrome differ in the type of interest they choose. The girls can develop an intense interest in dolls, animals, and fiction. Again, some of the interests are age- and gender-appropriate but unusual in their intensity. The interest in dolls can lead to a huge collection of dolls but a preference to play with dolls alone rather than with a peer. The doll play can include detailed re-enactments of scenes from television and the child's daily life. The interest in animals can be to such an intensity that the child acts being the animal, and if the interest is horses, may want to sleep in a stable. The interest in fiction can include collecting, and reading many times, the novels of a favorite author, and an interest in classical literature such as Shakespeare's plays and the stories of Charles Dickens or Mark Twain. This stems not from a desire to achieve success at school in English literature, but from a genuine interest in the great authors and their works.

## Adolescent interests

In the teenage years the interests can evolve to include electronics and computers, fantasy literature, science fiction, and sometimes a fascination with a particular person. All of these mirror the interests of peers, but, again, the intensity and focus is unusual. There can be a natural ability to understand computer languages, graphics, and advanced computer programming skills. The interest in fantasy literature and fantasy figures can be so intense that the person can develop their own role-play games and remarkably detailed drawing skills based on their special interest. There can also be a fascination with a particular character—mythical, historical, or real. When the interest is focused on a real person, it can be interpreted as a teenage "crush," although the intensity can lead to accusations of stalking and harassment.

## Why does the child develop a special interest?

Special interests may commence in association with, or response to, the experience of fear or pleasure. However, we are only just beginning to understand what may be the cause of the development of particular special interests. Several parents have described how an initial source or focus of fear can develop into a special interest. A fear of the toilet can evolve into a fascination with plumbing, an acute auditory sensitivity to the noise of a vacuum cleaner can lead to a fascination with the different types of vacuum cleaner and how they work, a fear of thunder become an interest in the weather. The child's intelligent and practical way of reducing the fear is to learn about the cause of his or her anxiety.

It is also fascinating that some interests are triggered by situations associated with a pleasurable experience. The interest is commemorative, linked to a memory of a pleasurable experience such as a visit to a theme park or science museum. Thinking about the interest can act as the "antidote" to negative thoughts or experiences. When we conduct an assessment of the pleasures in the child's life, children with Asperger's syndrome often value time engaged in their special interest more than almost any other pleasure. Any distraction or alternative activity is rarely as pleasurable. Another characteristic is that the child is almost mesmerized by the activity. This can be used as a means of preventing the intrusion of negative thoughts—a form of thought blocking.

## Reducing and using the special interest

While the motivation for the child with Asperger's syndrome is to increase their access to the interest, perhaps at the expense of other activities, the motivation for parents and teachers is to reduce the duration of the access to enable the child to engage in a wider range of activities. This is particularly important when the interest appears to virtually exclude social interaction with family members at home and peers at school, or affects the completion of homework assignments. What are the strategies that can reduce the time spent engaged in the interest? Can they serve a constructive purpose?

### CONTROLLED ACCESS

The problem may not be the activity itself but the duration and dominance over other interests. Some success can be achieved by limiting the time available using a clock or timer. When the allotted time is over, the activity must cease and the child can be actively encouraged to pursue other interests. Reassurance can be given that there will be another scheduled time for the chosen interest. The temptation to continue the activity will be quite strong, so the new activity may have to be in another room or outside. The replacement activity also needs to be something the child enjoys, even if it is not as enjoyable as the special interest. The approach is to ration access, and to actively encourage a wider range of interests.

Part of the controlled access program can be to allocate specific social or "quality" time to pursue the interest as a social activity. A parent or teacher has a schedule of regular times to talk about or jointly explore the interest. The adult ensures that they are not going to be distracted, and both parties view the experience as enjoyable. The author has found that such sessions can be an opportunity to improve his own knowledge of such interesting topics as the *Guinness Book of Records*, the Titanic, and weather systems. He is then able to talk with some authority and achieve respect from the children he meets with Asperger's syndrome. The conversation can become more reciprocal if the adults explain what they are interested in, and they can spend time exploring each other's interests.

## SUPPORTING MOTIVATION

Children with Asperger's syndrome have significant motivation and prolonged attention span when involved with their special interest. The treatment strategy is to incorporate the special interest in the classroom activity or to use access to the interest as a reward. For example, if the young child has an interest in Thomas the Tank Engine, there is a wide range of merchandise that incorporates the engines in reading books for different reading ages, mathematical activities, and writing and drawing. If the young child is interested in geography and flags in particular, he or she could count flags rather than the conventional items being counted by peers.

The interest can simply be used as a reward. Completion of allocated tasks in class results in free time to pursue the interest. For example, if he completes the ten sums within ten minutes, he has earned ten minutes on the class computer. Access to the interest is a remarkably potent reward. This strategy does require the teacher to be more flexible in the presentation of the class tasks, the curriculum, and reward systems. However, the benefits can be quite extraordinary to the child who can widen his or her knowledge base, demonstrate intellectual ability, and attain prizes and certificates of achievement.

Some parents have used the removal of access to the interest as a punishment for tasks not completed or misbehavior. While this strategy can be an effective component of a home-based behavior management program, it could become a trigger for aggressive behavior.

## A MEANS OF MAKING FRIENDS

"What makes a good friend?" For many children the reply is "We like the same things." Shared interests can be a source of friendship. I know a child with Asperger's syndrome who has a remarkable interest and knowledge regarding ants. His class peers tolerated his enthusiasm and monologues on ants, but he was not regarded as a popular choice as a companion. He was learning a range of friendship skills, such as waiting, sharing, compliments, and empathy. When he expressed these skills, they were achieved by intellectual effort and support and were perceived by others as somewhat contrived and artificial. He had few genuine friends. By chance, another child with Asperger's syndrome lived close by. He also has an interest in ants. There was an arranged meeting and the result amazed their parents and teachers. They were companions on ant-finding expeditions, made a joint ant study and regularly contacted each other with their latest ant-related discoveries. However, when observing their interactions, there was a natural fluency and quality to their social skills. They waited patiently, listened attentively, showed empathy, and gave compliments at a level not observed with their peers. Parents can consider some social engineering using the person's special interest to encourage prospective friendships. Local parent support groups can include the names and addresses of group members, but also the special interests of their son or daughter for the possibility of an arranged but potentially successful friendship.

## Can the signs become less conspicuous?

Yes, they can. The child with Asperger's syndrome has a brain that is wired differently. They do not have the intuitive ability to relate to their peers and manage their feelings, and do not have the same priorities and perception of the world as other children. However, over time—and with understanding, support, and guidance—the child can learn how to relate to others and achieve academic success. Any career is possible, from being a social worker to an engineer.

We must remember that there are two ways to acquire interpersonal skills: intuition or instruction. The child with Asperger's syndrome can learn what to do and say in order to achieve a successful career and personal relationships. It is possible to solve the social puzzle, using intellect and guidance.

## Chapter 7

# Anxiety and Obsessive-Compulsive Disorders

"Susan worries so much! All of us used to worry about a test the next day, but she worries about it for days in advance. In fact, she seems to worry about lots of things. She's even worried about *next* year. She tells me that it doesn't make sense, but she just can't help thinking about this stuff. I used to think that she avoided school because she just didn't like it. Now, I'm beginning to think that it's just too painful for her. In order to leave the house now for school, she goes through this little ritual of touching the door three times. It's just so sad to watch."

## Generalized anxiety disorder (GAD)

Anxiety disorders share the common thread of excessive worry and anxiety that exceed the person's ability to comfortably control them. "Anxiety" refers to the unpleasant sense of internal unrest, whereas "worry" refers to an apprehensive fear about *future* events.

According to the American Psychiatric Association's DSM-IV definition of Generalized Anxiety Disorder (APA 1994), the worries and anxieties must be sufficiently severe to interfere with functioning in life. The worries are about multiple things, occur most days, and feel difficult to control. In addition, there are physical symptoms such as insomnia, being tired, restless, feeling irritable or tense, or trouble concentrating.

Prevalence rates for GAD range from 2 to 9% for girls, and from 1 to 4% for boys (Bernstein and Layne 2004). Overall, there seems to be over-lapping roles of genetic temperament, parenting style, support systems, and life events in the development of GAD.

Children with GAD also have a two-thirds risk of having at least one of the other conditions of the syndrome mix described in this book, and these problems typically exacerbate each other. In particular, children with GAD have a one in four chance of having attention deficit hyperac-tivity disorder (ADHD) (Bernstein and Layne 2004).

According to the current theory of GAD, there is an imbalance in the loop between the brain's cortex and primitive centers for sensory input and emotion. Sometimes, these emotion centers get triggered without the conscious part of the brain even being "notified" why, leading to the (unfair) situation where we may experience nervousness, but not be con-sciously aware of what set it off.

Obviously, all of us worry to some degree. In fact, it would be hard to survive without some measure of worry. For example, why would we store extra food today if we weren't worried about being hungry during the winter? Why would we build a house now if we weren't worried about getting cold or wet? Why study if there was no test tomorrow? Indeed, there is an evolutionary advantage to appropriate amounts of worry.

So what is too much worry? We can distinguish generalized anxiety disorder (GAD) from normal childhood worries as follows:

- GAD kids worry about lots of things (six or more) at a time; typical kids only worry about one thing at time.

- GAD kids find the worry useless, unwelcome, and "alien"; typical kids may realize that small amounts of worry help them perform better.

- GAD kids usually *recognize* that they tend to worry more about things than their peers.

- GAD kids *anticipate* future events and worry about (or try to avoid) them well in advance; typical kids worry about *immediate* problems.

- GAD worries are stronger, more painful, and more disruptive. GAD kids worry about things that other children find trivial.

- GAD kids may have insomnia, poor concentration, irritability, or appear on edge.

- GAD kids often have bodily complaints such as headaches, abdominal pain, etc.

Sometimes, GAD kids can present as perfectionists. Although "perfectionism" is not recognized per se as a neuropsychiatric disorder, it certainly needs to be considered here as a type of anxiety. The school psychologist Dr. Kenneth Shore distinguishes between healthy striving for excellence and perfectionism as follows (Shore 2002).

Striving for excellence:

- Reaches for challenges.

- Derives pleasure from the process.

- Attributes success to hard work.

- A failure means weakness in one area.

- Celebrates accomplishments.

Perfectionism:

- Avoids challenges.

- Focuses mostly on the end product.

- Attributes success to luck.

- Failure means weakness as a person.

- Celebrates avoidance of failure.

In many nations, there has been a strong trend toward an increasingly educationally based and technologically driven culture. Contemporary society often places an extremely high premium on the value of education, more so than ever before. Now, many parents are preoccupied not just by trying to have their children attend college, but it must be a "good" college. Parents worry if their children will be able to support themselves. Unfortunately, this has all created a generation of young people who feel overwhelmed and pushed much of the time. These overscheduled and overly competitive children often do not get enough "down time," the value of which is often overlooked. Children need to learn to regulate themselves, and appreciate their own needs. A balanced lifestyle is harder to learn than might be imagined.

## Childhood anxiety is easy to miss

A striking feature of childhood anxiety is that often no one else knows about the problem. In fact, even the mothers of anxious children do not recognize the problem about half of the time (Berstein and Layne 2004)—a surprising statistic since mothers often know more about their child than the child does him/herself.

Interestingly, many children with anxiety disorders intuitively appreciate that they tend to "worry more about things than other children their age." Often, directly asking a child if she worries more than other kids will allow her to feel comfortable talking about it. The usual triggers are poor school performance (they feel less smart than classmates), a loss (death, illness), parental discord, witnessing violence directed toward themselves or others, or concerns over personal appearance (obesity, acne, height).

Sleep disturbances are an important physiologic window into anxiety disorders. Insomnia (defined as difficulty regularly falling asleep within 20 minutes after your head is on the pillow) is a very frequent symptom. Early morning awakening, such as at 3am, and difficult falling asleep again, are also common manifestations of anxiety. This may all lead to subsequent daytime sleepiness, which can contribute to poor school performance. (Note that loud snoring with obstructive sleep apnea can also cause daytime sleepiness and attention problems, but is not usually associated with insomnia.)

Since it is so easy to fail to recognize the anxiety disorder, we must always think about it when faced with a child who seems to only present with bodily complaints, avoidance, inattention, or irritability—and we frequently need to directly ask the child about it.

## Obsessive-compulsive disorder (OCD)

*Obsessions* are repetitive *thoughts* that are experienced by the person as unwelcome and basically senseless. The person feels compelled to try to ignore or neutralize the anxiety caused by these useless thoughts. (APA 1994).

*Compulsions* are the *behaviors* that the person feels obliged to carry out in order to ward off the anxiety caused by the obsessions. These behaviors—such as counting, touching, rechecking, or repeating words silently—are clearly excessive and unrealistic in their ability to head off the dreaded worry (APA 1994). For example, in order to ensure a safe bus ride, a child may feel the need to say "goodbye" exactly four times before she leaves the house. Logically speaking, though, this act won't really affect the safety record of the bus.

So, obsessions are thoughts, and compulsions are acts to neutralize the obsessions. The adult—at some point—recognizes that this is all unreasonable or excessive. Children may not reach this realization, and usually do not explicitly spell out obsessions or compulsions unless specifically asked about them. Note that these problems must be severe enough to interfere with the quality of life before a diagnosis can be made (APA 1994).

Anxiety or apprehension is at the root of the OCD loop. The person has a thought ➔ anxiety that the loop is happening again ➔ more thoughts. For example, an accountant might start to wonder if he made a mistake on a client's taxes. He knows that he did not actually make a significant mistake, but becomes afraid that these worries will keep coming back. The fear of ruining his whole weekend over these stupid worries makes him even more anxious, and the loop recurs.

Note that without the anxiety, there is no loop. In fact, an obsession is basically an irrational, recurrent anxiety. OCD and anxiety are part of a single spectrum.

## Treatment

### Inside the classroom

#### LET THE CHILD KNOW THAT YOU UNDERSTAND

If you are having trouble watching these obsessive-compulsive rituals, imagine how uncomfortable it must be to struggle with them directly. Let the child know that you understand how painful these issues can be. Just knowing that the teacher understands can be of great help.

Let her know that you recognize that by the time she gets to school, she may have already struggled with the stress of getting through her thoughts/rituals while trying to get to class on time. She may have stayed up late trying to perfect her work. There may have been fights between the child and her parents/siblings when she would not—or could not—comply with the others' needs. There may have been wrenching struggles over finding the "right" clothes, or with repetitive trips to the washroom.

### PROVIDE A SAFE, SUPPORTIVE ENVIRONMENT

Shore (2002) suggests the following strategies for perfectionist children—which can be extrapolated to the anxiety disorders.

- The class should be conducive to taking academic risks.

- All attempts at achievement should be celebrated—not just the successful ones.

- Make the classroom a safe haven where mistakes are expected.

- Make sure goals are realistic and explicit.

- De-emphasize grades.

- Use humor.

- Encourage students to trust their own judgment, which is a more useful skill in the long run than the short-term success that comes from double checking everything daily with the teacher.

- Teach "We all make mistakes—that's why they put erasers on pencils."

*Talk with the student* about their needs. Ask the student for their ideas as to how you can assist them. Dr. Leslie Packer (2005) suggests the following:

- Ask the child whether they would like to be kindly refocused when she appears internally distracted.

- Find out what things set off their worries/rituals, and work out ways to avoid those stimuli. For example, if trying to perfect handwriting is bothersome, then work out a practical solution—such as using a laptop, oral exams, providing breaks, or agreeing upon the amount of time for their written work.

*Accommodate quirks* when possible. As long as it does not interfere with other students or with safety, allow rituals that are beyond the child's ability to control. For example, if the child needs to call her parent at 11:03am, then you may need to allow it.

Recognize that *anxieties or OCD may silently interfere with work.* Sometimes, the anxieties or obsessions may cause silent, internal distractions. Keep an eye out for these hidden distractions as causes of the apparent symptoms of inattention, slow performance, or work avoidance. Alternatively, anxiety may cause excessive trips to the bathroom or school nurse.

Allow *extra time* as needed. Extra time may be necessary when:

- internal distractions slow the work

- it will alleviate anxiety associated with finishing "on time"

- it will accommodate for rituals, such as having to write perfectly, repeatedly erase, or exactly fill in the circles

Agree upon *limits for perfectionism*:

- Make a contract with the child to hand in work after an agreed upon limit of work time, or after a certain amount of re-checking.

- Avoid reinforcing the perfectionism that comes from praising it. Rather, reinforce reasonable effort and its resultant imperfections.

Work out an "*escape route.*" Pre-arrange that the child may leave the room when she feels the need. Perhaps a trip to the bathroom will resettle the nerves. Or, perhaps, a trip when needed to the school guidance counselor or psychologist might be agreed upon in advance.

*Educate peers* who are teasing the child. Children with anxiety disorders often try to hide their problems from their peers—a stressful process, at best. Even so, the rituals may be so uncontrollable that even friends cannot tolerate them. Have a session about accepting diversity, and educate fellow students about anxiety/OCD. The Obsessive Compulsive

Foundation at www.OCFoundation.org has materials. This would likely need to be done in consultation with the child and family.

## Professional treatment outside the classroom
### COGNITIVE BEHAVIORAL THERAPY

Often, the child can use his brain to override the anxieties. A counselor such as a psychologist usually provides this type of training. Skills might include the following:

- Gradually desensitizing the child to the anxiety through gradually increasing exposure to the feared stimulus/event.

- Avoiding "awfulizing," the process where one always exaggerates the importance of an event and expects an unreasonably horrible outcome. For example, a child may think that if he is late for school, he'll get an "F" and will no longer be able to go to college. He needs reminders that if he is late, then he'll get…a late slip. Not the end of the world

- Learning how to reframe one's attitude. For example, learning to see events as challenging opportunities rather than threats.

- Learning the process of thought blocking, where an intrusive thought is deliberately replaced by a pleasant one. For example, whenever the child is about to worry about a test, he is taught to instead imagine that he is relaxing at the beach.

Such cognitive behavioral therapies can be very effective for anxiety/OCD spectrum disorders.

### MEDICATION

The mainstays of possible medication treatment of anxiety/OCD disorders are the selective serotonin reuptake inhibitors (SSRIs) such as Prozac. They are remarkably helpful for this indication, and may make the strategies above more likely to be successful. Some authorities, though, worry that taking away the "pain" of the anxiety with medication may circumvent the child's desire to use the cognitive approaches above. See Chapter 14 for more on medications.

## Chapter 8

# Sensory Integration Dysfunction

## Martin L. Kutscher with Joelle Glick

"Jane, come over and look at this!! It's a great view from the top of the Empire State Building! If you come close enough to the edge, you can almost look straight down! Don't worry. The window will keep you from falling. You're perfectly safe."

Some of us seek such a thrill. Others will flee from it at any cost. All minds have equal rights, but all minds do not have the same response to stimuli.

### How the brain works (in four paragraphs)

The brain is a problem-solving machine. The problems come in the form of sensory input. Our brain collects that information from our sensory receptors, integrates it all, evaluates its importance, forms a plan, and executes our solution. Problem solved. It is time for the next one.

We are most familiar with our external sensory input—*sight*, *taste*, *hearing*, *touch*, and *smell*. There are also internal senses that regulate our bodies without our even being aware of it. These internal senses include *tactile sense*, which includes all the information that we process through our skin (such as being able to identify something we hold in our hand just by feeling it); *vestibular sense*, which monitors our position in space through gravity and motion; and *proprioceptive sense*, which informs us of our body position and body parts through the muscles, ligaments, and joints.

When stimulated, sensory receptors send an electrical current to the brain via a nerve. We only "know" what type of stimulus happened because the neurons from different sensory receptors go to different parts of the brain.

In addition to these objective reality reports that are sent to our brain, the brain's primitive limbic system also applies an emotional tag to each event. For example, some of us find that scrambled eggs evoke the memory of a nutritious, warm family breakfast. Some children find that scrambled eggs evoke from the limbic system the feeling of snake saliva. Everyone does not experience life in the same manner. We each have different ways of garnering information and reacting to it. Most of such sensory processing is subconscious. Only a selective portion is explicitly under our deliberate control.

## What is sensory integration dysfunction?
### Definitions

To begin with, *sensory integration* (SI) is defined as the process by which our brain interprets this information that we gather from our senses, and then outputs a meaningful response. For example, when someone pats you on the shoulder, your brain interprets the sensation of the hand on your back, and you turn around to see who it is. *Sensory integration dysfunction* is the brain's inability to process senses correctly. Some bits of sensory information get jammed up in a bottleneck, and certain parts of the brain do not get the sensory information they need to do their jobs.

Dysfunction occurs when one or more of the links in the sensory network are in disequilibrium.

- Intake by the sensory system. The brain takes in too much (called *hypersensitivity*) or too little (called *hyposensitivity*) sensory information. Hypersensitive individuals will avoid stimuli that excessively arouse them. Hyposensitive individuals seek out stimuli in order to arouse themselves. In either case, information is not received at the correct volume level.

- Organization by the nervous system. Sensory data is either not received, received inconsistently, or disconnected from the correct sensory messages.

- Output of movement, speech, or emotion. If the brain cannot efficiently process sensory messages, then meaningful and purposeful responses are lacking.

Sensory integration dysfunction has not been as well recognized by the medical community as the other disorders in this book. There is no medical classification of this disorder in the DSM-IV. Clinically, though, there do seem to be certain symptom complexes that really do exist. The following descriptions come largely from the landmark work, *The Out-of-Sync Child* by Sally Kranowitz (1998), which has made the whole area of SI dysfunction accessible to modern readers. See also 'Sensory Integration' in the Further Reading section.

### HYPERSENSITIVITY

The brain of a hypersensitive child registers sensations too intensely. For example, most of us find a friend's voice to be soothing. Imagine, though, if that voice came in at TOO LOUD A VOLUME, AND THERE SEEMED TO BE CONSTANT YELLING. Similarly, a child might be overwhelmed and run away from a light touch or a kiss on the cheek. He might defend himself from others, placing a physical barrier between himself and his surroundings in order to avoid stimuli. It is not unusual for hypersensitive children to respond to a minor scrape as if it were a life-threatening wound. They may even react to someone else's hurt feelings as if they were their own horrible experience. The hypersensitive child is often distractible because he is always paying attention to all stimuli, regardless of importance.

Sometimes, the threat of these stimuli to the child is easy to recognize. Other times, the child may not voice the problem, and it is subtler. All we may notice is that the child avoids certain situations, or may even seem inexplicably aggravated or irritated.

### HYPOSENSITIVITY

The brain of a hyposensitive child interprets sensations less intensely than normal. A typical hyposensitive child may be very "touchy feely" in order to satisfy his need for sensations. He may crash into objects or people because either he craves the sensation, he lacks proper motor control, or he does not perceive the sensation until it is too late to move out of the way. The hyposensitive child enjoys wallowing in the mud or hanging upside down. He might fall off a bike and then get right back on without crying. Many hyposensitive children will appear tired or sleepy. They might have trouble interpreting normal social, non-verbal cues. For instance, the child may not comprehend a parent's or teacher's scream. He might misinterpret another person's frown, and not react appropriately.

### WHAT ABOUT BOTH?

Some children exhibit both hypersensitive and hyposensitive characteristics. The brain of a child who displays both characteristics cannot correctly modulate senses. His over- and under-sensitivity to stimuli may depend on the time of the day or the nature and intensity of the stimulus. This child is often difficult to get under control because it is unclear how and when to help him.

## Common symptoms

Each child will have different symptoms depending on the type of SI dysfunction. For example, one child may be hypersensitive to touch and movement, while another child may be hyposensitive to touch and hypersensitive to movement. The following includes a list of common symptoms that occur under each category of SI dysfunction.

A child who is:

☐ *hypersensitive to touch, taste, or textures* might complain about discomfort caused by shirt tags, sock seams, turtlenecks, tight clothing, and rough-textured clothing; be a picky eater, preferring crunchy or soft foods, and disliking lumpy or sticky foods (tomato sauce or rice); refuse to have hair shampooed, combed, or brushed; withdraw from being touched; use fingertips (rather than the whole hand) to hold and investigate objects; avoid messy play with mud, sand, finger-paints, and glue

☐ *hyposensitive to touch, taste, or textures* may crave deep hugs; be unresponsive to cuts, shots, bruises, or scrapes; seem unaware of touch unless it is intense; be unaware of a runny nose, or a dirty mouth; fail to realize he has dropped something; appear aggressive around other children because he does not comprehend the pain that the other children are feeling

☐ *hypersensitive to movement* may dislike playground activities such as swinging, sliding, spinning, jumping, or climbing ramps, inclines, or jungle-gym equipment; feel uncomfortable while riding on an escalator or in an elevator; experience car or motion sickness; avoid taking risks, and appear slow moving or hesitant; have trouble learning how to climb or descend stairs or hills

☐ *hyposensitive to movement* might enjoy continuous and forceful swinging, hanging upside down, and spinning; appear fidgety in class, unable to stay in his seat; enjoy the scarier rides at amusement parks; fail to become dizzy after strong spinning; enjoy seesaws and trampolines more than other children.

A child who has:

☐ *low muscle tone* may have a floppy body; lay her head on the table, lie on the floor, or slouch in a chair; have difficulty opening doors; tire easily. (Note: low muscle tone, in this case, does not indicate a problem with the child's muscles. The child's brain, however, is not sending the correct information to the muscles to provide the proper support and tension for daily activities.)

☐ *poor fine motor control* might curl his hands in loose fists or put his hands in his pockets; have difficulty manipulating scissors, markers, and utensils; have trouble buttoning shirts; use gestures to communicate if he has poor fine motor control of his tongue and lips.

### SI DYSFUNCTION, ADHD, AUTISTIC SPECTRUM, AND LEARNING DISABILITIES

SI dysfunction, attention deficit hyperactivity disorder (ADHD), autistic spectrum disorders, and learning disabilities are separate but often coexisting disorders of the syndrome mix, which frequently elicit similar symptoms. A child might exhibit characteristics of ADHD or learning disabilities, but actually be suffering from SI dysfunction, and vice versa. Despite many "look-alike" symptoms, the hallmarks of SI dysfunction include a child's uncharacteristic behavior in response to touching, being touched, moving, and being moved.

Many children with autistic spectrum disorder have a significant degree of SI dysfunction. Some receptors are on incredibly "high gain," while others on "low gain." Loud noises, such as fireworks, may even trigger the equivalent of an anxiety attack. Some children who intermittently "toe walk" may suffer from a form of SI dysfunction due to a sense of discomfort regarding socks, or footwear.

## Getting professional help
### When and where

All of us have our likes and dislikes. That is totally normal. (As an example: "I don't like eggs.")

Sometimes, these likes and dislikes take on an unusual flair, but do not significantly interfere with function. We might call those "quirks." (For example: "I *never* eat eggs.")

At some point though, a person's likes and dislikes might cross the line and cause significant functional problems. (In this case: "I can't eat anywhere in the cafeteria because some of the other kids are eating eggs there.")

It is the latter group of problems—where likes and dislikes cause significant dysfunction—where the possibility of "sensory integration disorder" needs to be addressed professionally. The problems may be making the child miserable, or causing the life of people around him to be miserable.

In order to take advantage of the "plasticity" of a child's brain, significant sensory issues should ideally be identified early. Neural plasticity refers to the brain's capacity to change via the formation of new neuronal connections. The earlier the child gets help, the more likely he is to benefit from the treatment.

Observing good and bad behaviors at school and at home will help establish a pattern of the problem. Becoming aware of these patterns will be invaluable to yourself and the child. Make a chart of the incident, the time of day, and the child's complaint. This information will be extremely helpful in diagnosing the child and in determining a method for treatment.

Typical children build upon skills that they have learned and progress steadily into adulthood. Children with SI dysfunction, however, may need the guided support of an occupational therapist (OT) to help them acquire the basic foundation for proper sensory integration. The therapy seems to facilitate the development of the child's nervous system, although well-documented research in the area is scarce.

You can find an OT through your school system, your doctor, your nearest children's or local hospital, or from a professional organization such as the American Occupational Therapy Association (AOTA) or Sensory Integration International (SII). Not all OTs are trained in SI dysfunction.

## Screening and evaluation

### WHAT IS A SCREENING?

A screening is often a short, informal approach taken to check whether or not a child has acquired certain skills. A screening will often take place in a group setting, such as in a preschool. If any developmental problems have been suggested, the child's parents will be informed, and may be advised to get a full evaluation.

### WHAT IS A FULL EVALUATION?

A full evaluation entails a thorough, individualized session typically performed by OTs trained in the area. They evaluate the child with the help of standardized tests, strict observation of the child, and a questionnaire filled out by the parents that will help establish patterns since birth. The professional will establish what are the child's strengths and weaknesses; where, when, and how often they occur; and the intensity and duration of their occurrence.

The therapist will make a diagnosis, write a report, and confer with the parents. Sometimes, the conclusion might be that time is the only remedy needed. Suggestions for games and activities at home might also be discussed. Other times, the professional will suggest individualized therapy sessions for the child. Since each child is different, the activities that the therapist suggests will vary from child to child.

### IMPEDIMENTS TO THERAPY

It is difficult to do well-controlled, unbiased ("blind") research on the effectiveness of the varying treatments; and clear-cut medical proof of the effectiveness of occupational therapy for SI dysfunction remains elusive. It may be difficult to get school systems or health plans to cover unproven treatments. Therefore, everyone will need to weigh the benefits against the expenses.

Also, many children resist the therapy—which is often a type of gradual desensitization. After all, we are asking them to slowly expose themselves more and more to the noxious stimuli—a therapy that they did not ask for, that may be particularly unpleasant, and whose long-term benefits may not be at all apparent to the child as he goes through the treatments.

### OTHER TYPES OF THERAPY

Although most children with sensory integration dysfunction seem to benefit from occupational therapy, other more specific therapies might also be needed to help the problem. Some of these therapies include speech and language therapy, psychotherapy (if the child has become depressed and has a poor self-image), and physical therapy. Typically, physical therapy is used for gross motor problems or difficulties that involve the legs.

## Treatment activities for home and school

Caregivers should provide the child with a balanced "sensory diet"—a combination of activities that will specifically meet the needs of her nervous system. An experienced occupational therapist should individually develop and supervise an appropriate program. The child's safety should always be paramount. When initiating a program with an occupational therapist, remember the following:

1.  ***Structure the activities.*** Have certain times during the day (such as before or after mealtimes) when the activities will take place.

2.  ***Listen to the child.*** Let the child tell you which activities he wants. Allow him to tell you "more" or "less," but supervise carefully so that the child does not become overly aroused. Listen and watch for non-verbal clues during the activity to see which activities work the best.

3.  ***Anticipate.*** Anticipating how the child will react, and what the child wants, will enable you to better respond to his needs.

4.  ***Change the routine and environment.*** Periodically make changes for variety.

5.  ***Check with the therapist.*** The therapist will let you know if the sensory diet is adequately satisfying a child's needs.

The following menu of possible activities is adapted from Kranowitz (1998) and the sources listed in Further Reading.

*Alerting activities* for the *hyposensitive* child that seeks extra stimulation can include:

- eating crunchy foods, such as popcorn, pretzels, chips, crackers, carrots, celery, apples, ice cubes, gelatin, pudding, or mashed potatoes

- drinking liquids of varying temperatures or with bubbles (soda, seltzer)

- taking a shower

- jumping or bouncing.

*Organizing activities* will help the regulate the child's senses, for example:

- eating dried fruit, cheese, gum, granola bars, or bread crusts

- hanging from a bar by the hands.

*Calming activities* to help the *hypersensitive* child decrease hyper-responsiveness to sensory stimulation might include:

- sucking on a hard candy, pacifier, frozen fruit or ice cream bar, or a spoonful of peanut butter

- back rubbing or cuddling

- rocking or swaying slowly back and forth

- taking a bath.

Activities to develop *tactile integration* could include:

- water painting: give the child a bucket of water and a paintbrush and allow her to paint the porch, sidewalk, or herself with imaginary paint

- finger drawing: with your finger, draw different letters or shapes on the child's back, and have her guess what you drew

- sandbox: hide small objects in a sandbox and have the child feel around for the objects without looking

- bath time: let the child experiment with different textures by having her rub soaps (shaving cream, lotion) and sponges (loofahs, washcloths, and plastic brushes) on her skin; outside the bath, sprinkle powder onto the child, and brush or rub it into the skin; try having the child use an electric toothbrush

- reading: encourage the child to read books (with or without you) in a rocking chair or bean bag

- homework: use a dry erase board or a "magna doodle" to practice math and reading skills

- pets: allow the child to stroke a cat, brush a dog, or cuddle with a rabbit

- human sandwich: have the child lie face down on a gym mat; rub pretend mustard on the child (using firm, downward strokes) with a sponge, paintbrush, or washcloth; then fold the mat over the child, and press firmly up and down to squish out the excess "mustard"; the child will enjoy the deep, soothing pressure of this activity

- dress up: set up a box with various articles of clothing for the child to dress up in; include various textured clothing (satin, silk, velvet, leather).

Activities to develop *vestibular integration* might include:

- allowing the child to swing in a hammock

- walking on unstable surfaces: have the child walk on a sandy beach, a grassy area, or a waterbed—all situations that require the child to adjust his body as he moves

- swinging: encourage the child to swing; have her start on a swing where her feet touch the ground if she has a gravitational insecurity

- spinning: allow the child to swing on a merry-go-round or a tire swing; inside the child can use a swivel chair or a Sit 'n Spin

- sliding: see how many ways the child can go down a slide—sitting up, lying down, forward, and backwards

- swimming, horseback riding, and bowling: these will help develop the child's sensory integration

- therapy ball: have the child try to balance on a large therapy ball.

Activities to develop *proprioceptive integration* might include:

- housework: have the child carry grocery bags, laundry baskets, detergent, or loads of books; help the child push a vacuum cleaner; let the child help with digging or gardening

- pushing and pulling: let her push the stroller or a loaded wagon

- pillow crashing: pile a stack of pillows, cushions, or beanbag chairs, and have the child dive, roll, and burrow in the cushions

- bear hugs: give tight, soothing hugs to your own child

- meal preparation: allow the child to pour beans, rice, corn or water from a pitcher into cups or pitchers; carry pots, pans, and bowls; mix and then roll thick dough (to work muscles); use a meat mallet to tenderize meat

- playing catch: use a big ball or a pillow to play catch.

Activities to develop *fine motor skills* might include:

- flour sifting: lay out newspapers on the floor and provide flour, a scoop, and a flour sifter; allow the child to scoop and sift the flour

- blocks and puzzles: have the child work with Lego, building blocks, or a puzzle

- arts and crafts: provide scissors, markers, crayons, pencils, paint, paintbrushes, feathers, stickers, a hole puncher, pipe cleaners, buttons, beads, string, stamps, tape, and sparkles

- play dough: let the child manipulate the play dough by pounding, squeezing, kneading, rolling, and pinching it; have her flatten it into a pancake or roll it into a ball; provide objects that she can press into the play dough to make imprints (such as keys, coins, buttons, or paperclips).

Communication is key when it comes to increasing a child's success. Parents, classroom teachers, the principal, and the art, music, and gym teachers must all be aware of a child's problems. However, try to be positive and brief. Avoid terms like "hypersensitive to proprioceptive sensations" unless pressed for more specific information. Parents and teachers can share specific suggestions for the activities that work. For example, "My son is extremely sensitive to being touched. At home, he does best when he is not crowded. Could you keep in mind his need for space in the classroom?"

## Outcome

If a child has SI dysfunction, the problems will likely lessen but continue as the child grows. She will learn to compensate for her difficulties, but there will still likely be some struggle as she performs everyday tasks. However, with the proper attention to the problem, a person can be given the opportunity to experience the world more smoothly.

*Chapter 9*

# Tics and Tourette's

"That constant sniffling is driving me *crazy*! Some of the classmates find it so distracting, and a few are beginning to tease him about it. I know it's not his fault, but sometimes I feel tempted to ask him to stop. And why is he so nervous and always touching things?"

## Basic definitions
### What are tics?

Tics are rapid, repetitive actions that just happen to the child. They occur without any prolonged forethought by the person. Typically, tics tend to come and go, and change from one to another over time.

Tics are commonly classified into several types.

☐ *Simple motor tics.* "Motor" refers to the involvement of muscle movements. Common simple motor tics include simple movements such as eye blinks, nose scrunches, eye rolling, and neck thrusts.

☐ *Complex motor tics.* Complex motor tics involve movements that involve multiple groups of muscles. These might include body twisting, hopping, or shooting up of an arm.

☐ *Vocal tics.* These are tics that involve noises. Usually, the noise is a sniffling sound, throat clearing, squeak, bark, or echoing of what was just said. Only a small minority of patients with vocal tics actually have "coprolalia," which is the involuntary shouting of obscenities. Coprolalia should not be confused with simple cursing. Typical cursing is relevant to the current situation. In coprolalia, the taboo word occurs irrelevantly in the middle of a sentence. An example of coprolalia might be, "Could I please S-H-I-T have some maple syrup with my pancakes?" Sometimes, though, the coprolalia is just the blurting out of something socially totally inappropriate. For example, a person with a deformity might walk by and the result of coprolalia might be to shout out "Freak!"

In addition, tics can be classified as either *transient* or *chronic* (if they have occurred for at least a year, even if intermittently).

## What is Tourette's syndrome?

Simply defined Tourette's criteria include:

- a combination of at least two motor tics and at least one vocal tic

- symptoms have lasted at least one year

- onset before 18 years old.

Tourette's is basically just a mixed vocal and motor tic disorder. That's all. I have parents who tell me, "I've gotten comfortable with John's noises and movements. Just don't tell me he has Tourette's." Tourette's is not degenerative. It is nothing to be afraid of. Most people who have Tourette's probably do not even know that they meet the criteria.

## A complex problem

Having just simplified the definition of Tourette's, I must say that it is usually not nearly so simple.

Tourette's is a highly comorbid condition. Dr. Leslie Packer, a psychologist specializing in Tourette's, calls it Tourette Syndrome "Plus," to indicate that so many people with Tourette's have other conditions such as attention deficit hyperactivity disorder (ADHD), obsessive-compulsive disorder (OCD), anxiety, depression, or learning disabilities (see Further Reading section, p.214). For example, 60% of people with Tourette's have ADHD; conversely, 7% of people with ADHD have tics (Waslick and Greenhill 2004, p.492). The associated problems may be at least as debilitating as the tics themselves. Tourette's plays a major role in the syndrome mix.

Here are some medical facts (King and Leckman 2004, pp.709–715):

- Tics occur transiently in up to 18% of boys and 11% of girls.

- Tourette's syndrome occurs three to four times more often in boys than girls.

- A partial expression of Tourette's occurs in 1 out of 200 people.

- About 100,000 people in the U.S. have the full Tourette's syndrome.

- If one identical twin has Tourette's, then the twin sibling has a more than 50% chance of having Tourette's. This is a biological problem that then interacts with the environment to determine how strongly it will be expressed.

- OCD, anxiety, ADHD, and tics run strongly through the same families.

- Neuroanatomically, tics are due to a disorder in the planning loop between the cortex of the brain and deep-seated movement and sensory centers. This is the same loop involved in OCD/anxiety.

- Biochemically, tics seem related to too much activity by the neurotransmitters dopamine and norepinephrine.

## What about "nervous tics"?

Unless you already have the biological condition, stress does not cause tics. For people who are already prone to them, tics may be exacerbated by stressful situations. However, they are not caused by stress. Let's get rid of that misconception right away.

A medical analogy to migraines may help to explain. Stress may trigger a migraine in a person who is prone to them, but it would be crazy to say to a person who is seeing flashing lights with a severe migraine headache, "Hey, why are you reacting so badly to the stress that you are throwing up?" Stress may be the exacerbating factor, but then the natural condition takes over.

Actually, sometimes tics are maximal when the child is totally comfortable—such as when the child is at home watching television with his parents. It is important for teachers and parents to realize all of this, or they may misinterpret themselves as having created a stressed out child in a stressed environment.

## The natural course of tics

The only constant feature of tics is that they are variable. They come for no apparent reason, hang around for different amounts of time, go away, come back, never come back, or come back as a different type. Fluctuation and change are the norms. Tics seem to become maximal around 10–12 years of age. By late teenage years, many children are significantly improved, and half are essentially tic-free.

Infections may worsen the tics, especially streptococcal infection (a condition called PANDAS: pediatric autoimmune neuropsychiatric disorders associated with strep).

## Can people control their tics?

It is useless and counterproductive to ask a child to control his tics. It just does not work that way. After all, many people do not even know the tic is going to occur. It certainly is possible for some children to subconsciously suppress the tics temporarily (such as during the class play). Tics also tend to lessen when the child is engrossed in an activity, and during sleep. Some children learn to mask the tics by adding a more acceptable movement to the initial tic. For example, a sudden twitch of the arm may be masked by deliberately continuing the movement to brush the hair back.

However, there is little long-term conscious control over tics. The need to tic is irrepressible. It is like the need to breathe: a person can hold his breath for a while, but cannot do so indefinitely. So, can people exert control over their tics? Yes and no, but mostly no.

## Treatment and accommodations

As we have seen, tics are very frequently accompanied by other conditions in the syndrome mix. Keep a look out for those difficulties, and learn about them in the appropriate chapters.

## Understanding the child with tics
### IT IS OKAY TO NOTICE THE TICS

Tics are typically not a problem as long as nobody gives the child a hard time about them. I'm not suggesting that family, friends, and teachers be too stupid to notice them—just that they not make the child feel badly about them. No passing of judgment or teasing. Just acceptance. Fortunately, most people get so used to the tics so that they no longer notice them—a process called habituation.

### IT IS OKAY TO HAVE EMPATHY FOR THE TICS

When a child is having a problem such as tics, it may be helpful to let the child know that you recognize and legitimize the difficulty they are experiencing. They should know that someone is always available to talk about it, should they wish.

Dr. Packer has some "awareness exercises" on her website, which she suggests that caregivers try in order to understand what the child is going through (see the Further Reading section). For example, try to read a book while you twitch your head repetitively to the side every few seconds. Go ahead. Try it now while reading even one page. Distracting and annoying, isn't it? How would you like to live like that all day long? How would you like to go out in public while doing that?

So, empathy is good. Being available, when the child wants it, is good. However, bringing it to the child's constant attention certainly will not help, and is likely to be counterproductive.

### IT IS NOT OKAY TO BOTHER THE CHILD ABOUT THE TICS

Peers may ask why a child does those movements. That is a legitimate question. The child with Tourette's might then respond, "My brain makes me do that." Or "It's an allergy." Or maybe even, "I have Tourette's, which causes tics… No, not Lyme disease tics, but funny movements called tics. I'm seeing a doctor about it. Thanks for asking." Typically, the peer responds, "Okay, throw the ball!" That type of interchange is excellent. At times, though, peers tease the child. That is not acceptable.

## In the classroom
### EDUCATING CLASSMATES

In some cases, the parents or teacher may need to briefly educate the students about tics with an open discussion. It is harder to tease a child about something he already "admits" to. I've had some children who start the year with a presentation to the class about Tourette's. Be sure to discuss any public discussion of the problem with the child and the parents first. Dr. Leslie Packer gives some detailed pointers on such a presentation at her "Tourette Syndrome Plus" website (see the Further Reading section).

### TEASING MAY NOT BE THE ONLY PROBLEM

In general, then, tics are only a problem when other people make them so. There are, however, some kids for whom the tics will still be problematic.

- For some children, just the presence of the tics affects their self-image, even if no one else is giving them a hard time.

- Sometimes, tics interfere with daily activities. For example, constant neck or eye jerks may interfere with reading or cause neck pain. A constant cough may disrupt the child and the whole class.

- Sometimes the movements affect handwriting and or reading.

- Some children expend so much mental energy on the tics (either from trying to suppress them or from dealing with the embarrassment) that they may appear inattentive.

### SPECIFIC CLASSROOM ACCOMMODATIONS

Some of Dr. Packer's suggestions for accommodations for children with tics include the following:

- *The teacher should model acceptance of the tics*. If the teacher reacts negatively to them, what do we expect the students to do?

- *Allow the child to leave the room* if the tics become overwhelming. This may be especially important in quiet settings such as the library, study hall or assemblies.

- *Do not ask the child to leave the room.* That appears punitive for something over which the child has no control.

- *Provide extra time* if the tics slow down the work.

- *Provide creative accommodations* for difficulties. As an example, if reading aloud is embarrassing, consider avoiding it. If tics interfere with writing; then use oral tests, a scribe, or a computer.

- *Provide extra supervision if the child is being teased* in situations such as recess or lunch.

- *Allow preferential seating.* Some children with tics prefer to sit in the back of the class so that no one can see the tics.

## Medication

For most children with moderate tics, life will be okay with simple education, understanding, and reassurance about the condition. When the tics remain a significant problem in a child's life, then we may need to add medication to the regimen. Medications do not cure the symptoms; they just control them for the days that the child takes them. Put another way, there is no long-term medical harm if we hold off on medication. We will not have to kick ourselves and say, "Oh, if we had only started medication earlier." Starting earlier would have had no effect on the tics today.

The critical questions, then, as to starting medication are:

- is the issue a quirk or a problem? It is a problem when the tics diminish the child's self-esteem or function

- is the problem worth the possible side-effects of medication for this child, at this point in time?

The commonly used medications to treat tic disorders are as follows:

- Catapres (clonidine) or Tenex (guanfacine) are frequently the mediations tried first. They may help the tics, and may help any co-occurring ADHD (particularly the impulsive part). The most common side-effect can be sedation.

- Risperdal (risperidone) and other "neuroleptics" are usually quite effective for tics, and may help control angry or aggressive behaviors as well. They do not help inattention. Common side-effects include sedation and weight gain. There are also rare, potentially serious, side-effects.

Note that the stimulants used to treat ADHD can at times alter the frequency of the tics. See Chapter 14 on medications for more information.

# Chapter 10

# Depression

"I just don't know what has happened to Jane. She has so little energy! That twinkle in her eye is gone. Nothing seems to motivate or excite her anymore. Sometimes she can be so irritable, and yells at me over nothing. Sometimes, she curls up in a ball and can't get up. Then she can't fall asleep at night, or wake up in the morning. She's always late. Her eating habits are all off, too. We thought it might be mono or Lyme, but her tests just came back negative.

"She tries to put on a brave face at school, but her grades are slipping. Her absences from school make it worse—she can't possibly catch up. She won't go in for extra help. 'Why should I?' she says. 'They don't understand, and can't help me anyway.'"

## Defining depression and dysthymia

The American Psychiatric Association makes the distinction between a major depressive episode, which is a severe, typically episodic illness; versus dysthymia, which is a more smoldering condition.

□ *A major depressive episode* is marked by the experience *nearly every day for at least two weeks* of feelings of sadness, emptiness, or loss of "zest." Daily activities no longer hold any interest or pleasure. There may be feelings of worthlessness or guilt, and recurrent thoughts of death may occur. The ability to concentrate or make decisions may be altered. Before adulthood, this may all manifest simply as irritability. In addition, there are physical symptoms of depression, including sleep problems, fatigue, restlessness, loss of energy, or unintentional weight loss. All of these problems must cause actual dysfunction in a person's life for at least two weeks in order to make a diagnosis of a major depressive episode (APA 1994).

☐ *A dysthymic disorder* is defined as depression *for more days than not over a two-year period* (although children/adolescents are only required to be irritable for at least one year). There may be physical symptoms as seen in a major depressive episode. Over this period, the symptoms never resolve for more than two months, and cause functional impairment in the person's life (APA 1994).

Mood disorders can appear differently through the lifespan. Younger children may be unable to verbalize their sadness. Instead, the only symptoms that caregivers may notice are irritability, getting into fights, or avoidance. Alternately, they may present with physical symptoms such as headaches or abdominal pain. Older children and adolescents may present with the more typical core symptoms of sadness and emptiness along with loss of motivation, loss of energy, and loss of self-esteem.

## Real-life symptoms

Depression in children is easy to miss. Children under age seven in particular, may be unable to directly state their sadness. Thus, we need to keep an eye out for an expanded range of symptoms.

- *Sadness*—"Mommy, I hate feeling so down! I just feel so empty and hopeless." I've really got a pretty good life. Why do I feel this way?

- *Feeling of emptiness*—"I just feel so, so, so alone."

- *Self-esteem problems*—"I'm just no good at anything! I'm so stupid!"

- *Withdrawal/loss of interests*—the mother bemoans about her child, "Sleep. Do nothing. Sleep. I can't get him to do anything except just hang around."

- *Irritability*—"Jane just walks around with a chip on her shoulder. For no reason, she's just always in a lousy mood. My son John—the one with ADHD [attention deficit hyperactivity disorder]—is usually happy as a clam as long as I leave him alone. He snaps at me when I make a demand on him like coming to dinner. My depressed child, though, just walks around looking miserable. She snaps at me even if I leave her alone."

- *Bodily complaints*—"Jane is always complaining about headaches, or maybe her stomach is hurting her. I've been to lots of doctors. We've had MRIs [magnetic resonance imaging] and blood tests. They tell me it's just stress."

- *Sleep problems*—"Jane can't seem to fall asleep. She is always worrying about something. Sometimes, she naps all afternoon. We can't get her up in the morning, so she's always late for school."

- *Appetite problems*—"She keeps eating and is getting fatter. No wonder she is so depressed!" The last thing that a teenager with depression needs is the additional problem with self-image that comes from being overweight. Loss of weight can also accompany depression.

- *Concentration problems*—"I don't get it. She never had trouble concentrating before." If concentration problems suddenly begin in the later school years, we need to be suspicious about diagnosing ADHD. New onset attention problems suggest another issue, such as depression, anxiety, drug use, etc.

- *Stress on the family*—"I can't bear to see my child like this!" First, the child's lack of effort—along with his irritability—is exceptionally hard to live with. Even more difficult, though, is watching your child be unhappy. What could be worse?

- *Stress on the teacher*—"I went into teaching to get kids excited about this subject. But I can't seem to get this kid involved. I offer her help, but she never takes it. She doesn't even seem to try." What could be worse for a teacher than to have a student who is unable to muster any motivation?

- *Thoughts of death*—the horrific truth is that suicide is a leading cause of death in adolescents. We all need to be vigilant, and take any talk of self-harm seriously.

## Neurobiology of depression

Like many behavioral problems, depression is often a combination of environmental effects on a predisposed brain. One marker that this emotion is due to a biological illness (rather than just being "weak in spirit") is that biologically depressed children often know that their feelings of sadness don't make sense. Their feeling of sadness feels unwelcome, unacceptable, and imposed upon them. Sometimes, though, the depressed child does lose objective reality and truly feels that her life is actually horrible. Of course, sometimes, the life she is living *is* truly horrible.

On a biochemical level, depression seems due to a largely genetic dysfunction of the right parietal-temporal cortex stemming from:

- too little of the neurotransmitter norepinephrine released by nerves in the locus coeruleus (part of the brainstem) onto the cortex; and

- too little of the neurotransmitter serotonin released by the median raphe (also part of the brainstem) onto the cortex.

The role of certain hormones is also being investigated.

## Treatment
### Counseling

Counseling is typically part of the treatment. In order for therapy to even be successfully started, the child must:

- recognize that there *is* a painful problem; otherwise, what is there to talk about?

- recognize that the child has a role in that problem; otherwise, why should the child see the therapist? If—in the child's mind—the parent or teacher is the one with the problem, then *they* should be having the counseling!

## Adjusting the school environment

Parents need to bring the school in as part of the team. Unfortunately, there is frequently such a stigma attached to "psychiatric disorders" that no one tells the teachers about the problem. Left in the dark, the teacher often feels no recourse other than to either come down hard on the child or give up on her. But there is much that can be done to help at school.

- *Teachers need to allow time to make up for missed work.* Children with depression often miss a lot of school. Don't expect the child to seek out the extra help himself. He's depressed.

- *Don't consider the lack of effort to be a deliberate choice.* Loss of motivation is a cardinal symptom of depression.

- *Try to avoid the vicious cycle of depression→ school failure→ more depression.* We don't want to let academic problems exacerbate the underlying depression.

- *Accommodate poor attention span during depressive state* (see Chapter 3 on ADHD).

- *Children with depression may be physiologically unable to get up in the morning.* Such medically related tardiness will need to be excused, and the school schedule adjusted to fit the child's needs.

- *Consider school issues that may have triggered depression in the first place.* In particular, it is not uncommon for bright, appealing, inattentive girls with ADHD to go undiagnosed until high school. After so many years of being told that they could do better, things finally fall apart and depression sets in. Always be vigilant for one condition in the syndrome mix causing, mimicking, or exacerbating the symptoms of another condition.

- *Talk of suicide should be taken seriously.* Parents and therapists should be notified immediately.

## Medication

Given the biochemical underpinning commonly involved with depression, it makes sense that medication often plays a key role in treatment.

The mainstay of antidepression medication is a class called the selective serotonin reuptake inhibitors (SSRIs). These medicines inhibit the removal of serotonin from the synapse, leading to raised serotonin levels. Despite use for over a decade in children, only a few controlled studies have been done in that setting. Roughly, a half to two-thirds of children have a significant beneficial effect from the SSRIs. The medications may take one or two months to take effect. If one SSRI does not work or is not tolerated, another one may be tried. Note that the SSRIs can worsen bipolar depression, and may have other side-effects as described in Chapter 14. Although other SSRIs are often specifically used, only Prozac actually has U.S. Food and Drug Administration approval for use in children with depression.

Before the introduction of the SSRIs, the mainstay of treatment had been the tricyclic antidepressants such as Elavil, Tofranil, or Pamelor. Multiple controlled studies have shown that the tricyclics do not work in childhood depression.

Other medications include Wellbutrin and Effexor. These and the other medications are discussed in Chapter 14.

Overall, it may take months to find the correct dose of the correct medication; and even then, medication may not help.

## Outcome

Depression is extremely common. At any given time, some 1–4% of children will be experiencing major depression. Overall, some 15–20% of kids will have a major depressive episode before becoming an adult (Weller, Weller and Danielyan 2004). That is a lot of children. That probably means the average teacher has taught lots of depressed students, without knowing it.

The good news is that some 90% of children with depression will go into remission within a year. The bad news is that up to a half will have a relapse (Weller *at al.* 2004).

Depression is an incredibly terrible, empty feeling. It is horrible. It needs to evoke from us an incredibly empathic response.

## Chapter 11

# Bipolar Depression

"I'm really scared… It's like he's possessed. One minute he is the sweetest, kindest person. He would do anything for you. Then, for no reason, something sweeps over his brain and he turns on me. There's screaming and yelling and things flying around the room. Once he gets going, his rages may take hours. He can be irritable and moody for days on end. Sometimes, he's so down that I'm afraid for his own safety—not to mention my own. Sometimes, though, he's so 'up' that his judgment gets really poor. Where does he get off thinking that he's going to be a senator one day! And, it always seems to be worse when he's at home. When I tell people about it, they look at me like *I'm* crazy. My father-in-law was manic-depressive, and it led him to a drinking problem. I'm so scared…"

"Bipolar depression" (BD) is the scientific name. "Manic depression" is the old name. "Bipolar disorder" is becoming the politically correct name. Call it what you will, it can be a horror. It can make the rest of the conditions in this book look like playtime. The mood changes that take the brain hostage—both up and down—are frightening, confusing, and often dangerous. To make matters worse, people with BD are at a hugely high risk for comorbid conditions of the syndrome mix.

## What is bipolar depression?

"Bipolar" refers to a mood disorder that rapidly shifts between the poles of two extremes: depression (sad mood) and mania (grandiose, high mood). Indeed, bipolar depression is marked by a life of extremes, in general. There may, though, be short or long periods of relative normalcy.

Hallmarks of BD include the following:

- *Depressive episodes* marked by sad, flat, down, empty, hollow feelings where nothing seems to matter or be exciting; appetite and sleep may be altered. (See Chapter 10 on depression for more details.)

- *Manic episodes* marked by a high mood. There are expansive, unrealistic, disorganized, and grandiose behaviors. During a manic episode, the person may appear pressured and over-talkative. Her ideas may be loosely connected. In adults, typical mania might include grand schemes such as a sudden shift of careers, or shopping sprees. Like a spinning hurricane, the uncontrolled energy of a manic storm can leave a huge wake of bewilderment and destruction.

- *Extreme irritability*, which is the typical form of mania in children, or may be a sign of a depressive spell.

- *Very goal-directed behavior*, often to the detriment of other needs.

- *Poor judgment.*

- *Extreme rages that may last for hours*. Older patients may have more obvious cycles of these events.

- *Extreme sensitivity to stimuli.*

Other symptoms of BD may include:

- little sleep requirement
- extreme craving for sweets
- extreme fear of death
- extreme sexuality

- oppositional or obsessive traits

- hallucinations

- suicidal tendencies

- substance abuse risk

- bedwetting

- severe separation anxiety

- precociousness as children.

Typically, most of the symptoms are shown primarily at home—as if the parents did not feel badly enough already. Parents may be surprised to hear that their child is a little angel at school; teachers may be surprised to hear that the child is so difficult at home.

Notice how often the word "extreme" is used in BD. Read *The Bipolar Child* by Dimitri Papolos for more details (see the Further Reading section).

## Confusion with other conditions

Bipolar depression is a great masquerader. It continues to be frequently under- or misdiagnosed. Once again, conditions can co-occur, or can be confused with or exacerbate each other. A host of neuropsychiatric conditions turn out to be associated with BD, such as attention deficit hyperactivity disorder (ADHD) and disruptive behavioral disorders, as well as trouble with the law and substance abuse (Weller *et al.* 2004).

Consider BD rather than ADHD (or in addition to ADHD) when there are the above symptoms or:

- a strong family history of bipolar disorder or substance abuse.

- prolonged temper tantrums and mood swings (in BD, the angry, violent, sadistic, and disorganized outbursts can last for hours, versus typically less than 30 minutes in ADHD)

- bipolar rages arising typically from parental limit setting (versus ADHD rages which are usually from over-stimulation)

- walking around with an angry "chip on your shoulder" (BD people often walk around looking miserable for no apparent reason. In ADHD, the kids are typically quite chipper up until the moment that someone/something frustrates or overwhelms them. To put it another way, depressed people are irritable; ADHD people are easily irritated.)

- oppositional and defiant behaviors

- "intentionally" aggressive, explosive, or risk-seeking behaviors

- symptoms that worsen with stimulants (such as Ritalin)

- morning irritability that may last hours in BD (versus minutes in ADHD)

- separation anxiety, bad dreams, disturbed sleep; or fascination with gore

- you never know what child you are going to get today.

## Bipolar in children

BD typically begins in late teen or early adult years. It had been thought to occur primarily in adults, but is now increasingly being recognized in children as well.

There are some significant differences in symptoms depending upon the person's age. In adults, it typically takes days or months between switching moods. In children, the moods can alternate ultra-rapidly—up to several times per day; or, perhaps, even occur simultaneously. Also, in children, the manic stage is more typically marked by *irritability* rather than by euphoria.

## Treatment

First, follow the suggestions in Chapter 2 on the general principles of treatment. All of the suggestions apply particularly to bipolar. Go ahead... Re-read that chapter... We'll still be waiting right here. Tap. Tap. Tap...

## In the classroom

Bipolar is *overwhelming*. The key is to "underwhelm" by keeping it predictable, calm, and secure. Can you imagine what it must be like to have unexpected, monsoon-sized, tidal waves of inexplicable emotion sweep over you? These children need a reliable, soothing environment. Many of these suggestions could be used by good teachers for all students.

- *Make routines predictable.* Let everyone (child and parents) know about weekly assignments such as spelling tests. Consider keeping a schedule of the day's events on the blackboard.

- *Give adequate notification before making transitions.* Make sure that the child actually hears and processes these warnings—he may be preoccupied.

- *Give extra time for transitions.* Allow him to finish a task before moving on. Failure to do so may prove extremely frustrating, and the precipitation of a meltdown does not help anyone.

- *Allow plenty of breaks,* both planned and as needed.

- *Arrange "secret" hand codes* that the student can give to the teacher to indicate present or impending moods. (e.g., thumb up means "good," five outstretched fingers means "stressed," etc.)

- *Allow—and encourage use of—a minute to reflect* before the child makes his choice.

- *Allow the child to pull back* when he feels overwhelmed—with no hassling questions. Let the child go to the bathroom, for a drink of water, or to a pre-selected place or person which functions as a safe haven. These types of pop-off valve activities should be arranged in advance of their need. School safety policies need to be considered.

- If *classroom commotion* is a de-stabilizing force for the child:
  - have the child sit preferentially in a quiet part of the room
  - have the child sit next to calm, quiet students.

- Some students may not tolerate *lunchroom or recess noise.* They may need an aide at those times, or spend those periods elsewhere.

- *Avoid direct confrontation!!!* (See Rule 2 in Chapter 2, p.36.) If certain activities trigger meltdowns, then try to steer clear of them. For example, if a child screams before going to music class (maybe he has a sensory integration problem?) then don't take him there. A useful tactic is to offer a child two acceptable alternatives to choose from.

- *Some bipolar kids need an aide.* It's hard to stop class and publicly come over to a child who is "losing it." An extra aide in the class can quietly come over and intervene while the main teacher goes on with the lesson. Sometimes, the child will need her own aide—although some older children, in particular, will not tolerate that. Other children might be candidates for an "inclusion" class, in which case several special-need children share an aide or special education teacher in a class of otherwise "typical" children. Hopefully, the extra helpers will have some training in dealing with the particular set of problems faced by the child.

Bipolar children also need lots of positive support!

- *Say something nice* every five minutes. Say 12 nice things for every negative comment. Find *something* nice to say, even if it's just saying, "Billy, I like the way you merely yelled at Tommy, rather than bopping him on the head."

- *Teach other students to accept diversity.* Teach peers how different brains can learn and react differently.

Remember, too, that punishing a bipolar child for a rage attack makes as much sense as punishing a child who has epilepsy for having a seizure. Do not punish children for behavior that is out of their control. It is neither fair nor useful. And, again, federal law in the U.S. prohibits punishing children for their disability.

A child's *rapport with a teacher* can make or break a school year. Teacher traits that are beneficial to the special needs child include:

- flexibility (Do not get involved in power struggles. Give *palatable* alternatives. Threats and ultimatums can set off the child into making poor choices.)

- patience

- sense of humor

- being receptive to suggestions from others.

Don't *underestimate* your role in a child's success, and don't necessarily *overestimate* your role in a child's failures.

### COMMUNICATION BETWEEN SCHOOL AND PARENTS

Caregivers should share amongst themselves:

- what strategies work, and just as importantly, what strategies don't work

- what is happening in their sphere, because it may spill over into the rest of the child's life

- what academic areas need more work, and which are causing stress or taking too much time

- what times of day make the most sense for particular activities—during the course of the day, there are likely to variations in a child's attention, frustration tolerance, or medication effects.

Feedback about medication effects is essential. Teachers and parents are the eyes and ears for the physician. Doctors completely depend on the feedback that they receive. We cannot judge a medication's "real-world" effectiveness while the child is in the office. Giving feedback is not a presumptuous imposition; it is essential. When presented in a helpful manner, such feedback is usually well taken by everyone. Doctors need to know:

- Does the medicine work?

- Does the medicine's effectiveness have peaks and valleys?

- Are there side-effects, such as sleepiness, agitation, or increased appetite?

- Does the child need allowance for extra snacks or water breaks?

Caregivers should communicate *directly* with each other. Many children with BD may not be accurate historians as they relate their trials and tribulations between parents and teachers—especially those kids who also have oppositional defiant disorder (ODD).

- Direct communication eliminates the unreliable middleman.

- Use a phone, e-mail, or a journal that goes back and forth with the child's backpack.

### DEALING WITH MANIC SPELLS

The life of a child with BD is plagued by mood swings. No one—not the child, the parent, or the teacher—knows what kind of kid is going to show up today. Some days, the child will be manic, with either expansive energy or irritability. Suggestions for handling such behavior include the following:

- Allow the children physical outlets for their driven energy. Let them be the ones to hand out and pick up paper, wash the board, or to deliver the attendance list to the office. Allow them to get up and use the computer.

- Direct them to productive hands-on projects.

- Help them set realistic goals, with reasonably sized projects.

### DEALING WITH DEPRESSIVE SPELLS

- See Chapter 10 on depression.

- Let them know you understand.

- Allow medically related morning tardiness. Depressed children may have physiological trouble waking up in the morning.

- Talk of suicide should be taken seriously. Parents and therapists should be notified expediently.

- Accommodate their poor attention during mood swings.

### CLASSIFY THE CHILD AS "OTHERWISE HEALTH IMPAIRED"

The Children and Adolescent Bipolar Foundation recommends "Otherwise Health Impaired" (OHI) as the most appropriate special education category for BD students. This categorization validates that bipolar is a true medical health condition. Unfortunately, the alternative classification is "emotional disability" (ED). ED seems to imply that the child's behavioral problems are "emotional," i.e., that they somehow are due to poor upbringing and never bothering to learn basic appropriate behavior—a clearly counterproductive model. BD children may also merit other classifying labels, such as learning disabled, ADHD, and ODD.

## ADDRESSING SPECIFIC PROBLEMS

Deal with typically associated learning problems. Many children with BD have problems in the areas of:

- attention
- organization and analysis of learned material
- problem-solving skills
- memory and recall of learned material
- medication side-effects, such as sedation or even mild cognitive slowing.

Address problems in social interactions. BD kids may have problems with social interactions that may benefit from:

- social skills classes
- rehearsal of appropriate responses in advance of typical problems (Set up mock stories and act/write out productive responses. Discuss "what if" scenarios.)
- private discussion about inappropriate responses after the problem occurs.

Accommodate associated attention deficits. Children with bipolar disorder are at extremely high risk for having co-occurring ADHD as well (Weller et al. 2004). Even without ADHD as an additional primary diagnosis, the child's attention span may worsen during manic or depressive episodes. See Chapter 3 on ADHD, and consider doing the following:

- Decrease the workload (e.g., do four out of five problems). Focus on quality rather than quantity.

- Give extra time for tests and schoolwork.

- Check in on their progress frequently, and give positive prompts.

- Have them sit near the teacher.

- Avoid excessive classroom heat, or dim lights, that may interfere with attention.

## Medication

The complicated issue of treating bipolar depression is addressed in Chapter 14 on medication. In general, medications will be an integral part of the treatment. Sometimes, though, their side-effects can be significant.

## Chapter 12

# Oppositional Defiant Disorder

A four-year-old boy was told by his nursery school teacher that he had to lie down on his cot at rest-time. The boy said that he was not going to lie down. The teacher insisted upon compliance. The boy calmly walked over the cot, urinated on it, and announced, "I guess that I don't have to lie down on it, now." This true story was the harbinger of future oppositional behaviors.

## What is oppositional defiant disorder?

This is an unpleasant chapter. Throughout the rest of the book, it is fairly easy to take the child's side—at least during a calm moment. Oppositional defiant disorder (ODD) may commonly have a biological underpinning, but the behaviors seen in this condition test the limits of our ability to exercise empathy.

ODD is marked by aggressive, spiteful, vindictive, and sometimes remorseless behavior. There is a persistent pattern of actively refusing to follow requests (not just being too overwhelmed at the moment to comply), over-reactions, easily losing one's temper, and being annoyed. Children with ODD may deliberately annoy other people, and argue with adults. Often, there is failure to take responsibility for one's own actions. In order to diagnose ODD, these symptoms must be excessive for the child's age, and cause a functional disturbance (APA 1994).

ODD is rarely seen in isolation. Rather, this type of behavior is usually a symptom complex resulting from some other underlying disorder of the syndrome mix. Personally, I rarely make a primary diagnosis of ODD. Usually, the negative behaviors tend to improve with the treatment of the underlying problem(s).

## Types of disruptive behavioral disorders

ODD is the least severe of the three types of disruptive behavioral disorders. Full definitions can be found in the DSM-IV (APA 1994).

☐ *Oppositional defiant disorder (ODD)*. ODD children are unwilling to conform (even with an intriguing task). They may be negative, deliberately annoying, or argumentative, angry, and spiteful. They seem to get a "charge" out of giving other people a hard time.

☐ *Conduct disorder (CD)*. Children with CD are more frequently overtly hostile and law breaking, with a lack of remorse. These people violate the rights of others, such as with physical cruelty to others or animals, stealing, etc.

☐ *Antisocial personality disorder*. People with antisocial personality disorder have a pervasive pattern of severe violation of the rights of others, typically severe enough to merit arrest.

Fortunately the vast majority of the disruptive behavioral disorders fall into the ODD group. The others—conduct disorder and antisocial personality disorder—are beyond the scope of this text.

## ODD through the lifetime

About 5–15% of school-age children meet criteria for ODD. By puberty, the prevalence of ODD in girls catches up to the prevalence in boys (Tynan 2003).

As infants and toddlers, the ODD child may display irritability, stubbornness, rigidity, aggression, intense reactions, and tantrums. Sometimes, these behaviors are worsened by inconsistent or excessively harsh parenting techniques, or by family stresses. Behavioral symptoms may be so dominant that other underlying problems (such as learning difficulties) may be overlooked.

By school age, symptoms spill over to impact teachers, other adults, and peers. Aggression and other poor social skills lead to increasing rejection and attention-seeking behaviors. The children often misinterpret peer actions. Lacking the social and verbal skills to solve the problem, they may become physically aggressive. ODD children often do not see their own role in the problem, frequently blaming others instead. This failure to take responsibility for their actions is a further source of bewilderment and anger for those around them. As the child ages, the earlier symptoms of open defiance may be accompanied by covert activities such as stealing or lying.

Even with maximum intervention, this symptom complex may be difficult to correct—an aggressive toddler is more likely to be an aggressive adult. Those children with particularly intense symptoms as toddlers, and for whom behaviors worsen through early childhood, are at greater risk for developing a more severe conduct disorder in later years. Parental strife, exposure to abuse, and substance abuse can exacerbate the problems.

## Relationship with other disorders

ODD is really a symptom complex that possibly can be diagnosed by itself; but more typically occurs in the setting of other diagnoses, such as attention deficit hyperactivity disorder (ADHD), bipolar depression (BD), depression, or anxiety.

## ODD and ADHD

In fact, 50% of ADHD children are said to have disruptive behavioral disorders (Tynan 2003). Even in the absence of a full diagnosis, the lives of many children with ADHD are afflicted by lying, cursing, taking things that do not belong to them, blaming others, and being easily angered or annoyed.

This frequency is not surprising given the executive dysfunction seen in so many ADHD children. ADHD people have trouble inhibiting their behavior, trouble anticipating consequences, and trouble learning from their mistakes. No wonder, then, that they keep bumping unpleasantly into other people. Typically, though, we get the sense that these problems are happening "to" the ADHD child. Also, the negative behaviors tend to be more impulsive in ADHD than with ODD. For example, an ADHD child may curse when called for a delicious dinner that his parent has made for him. Most likely, that stems from being overwhelmed with the frustration of making a transition. In ODD, the negative behaviors seem "deliberately" designed just to achieve the thrill of being negative or difficult. An ODD child would curse when called for dinner because he really intends to worsen the life of his parents—to the degree that a child can be blamed for "intending" anything.

In addition, children with ADHD are usually remorseful (at least, later) compared to ODD kids.

Most children—including those with ADHD—instinctively choose to please others when they can. When the negative behaviors such as lying come simply from being overwhelmed, or from the inability to get past the current frustration, I tend to classify them as part of the expanded spectrum of ADHD symptoms. Defined this way, I personally classify relatively few children with ODD.

## ODD and depression, anxiety, OCD, and BD

Depressed and anxious children may suffer from episodes of very threatening low self-esteem. When demands are places upon them, they may feel "backed into a corner." Their overwhelmed nervous system responds with the "fight or flight" reaction. For children with autistic spectrum disorders, anxiety is often such a trigger of oppositional behaviors. Once again, we see that conditions in the syndrome mix can cause and exacerbate each other.

## Treatment

There are some commonsense interventions that parents and teachers can use to ameliorate the symptoms of ODD.

- *Evaluate and treat associated problems* such as ADHD, bipolar depression, depression, OCD/anxiety, autistic spectrum disorder or learning disabilities that can underlie or worsen the problem. THIS IS CRITICAL.

- *See the suggestions in Chapter 2*—in particular, Rule 2:
  - Pick your battles.
  - Head off fights before they happen.
  - Stay calm!
  - Do not engage in "discussion" with an out-of-control brain (yours or the child's.) Wait until tempers have abated.

- *Don't show negative emotions* to the child's behavior. That just reinforces it. Either ignore the child's negative comments, or calmly hand out the previously established punishment for the infraction.

- *Decide how you will respond to problems before they occur.* The planned response is much more likely to be reasonable and helpful than a response made in the heat of the moment (Chandler n.d., see Further Reading).

- *Choose reasonable punishments* that actually teach a lesson, and that can actually be enforced.

- *Find something positive* to praise and focus on. Reward flexibility and cooperation.

It is also important to take care of yourself (with good sleep, eating, and fun times for yourself) and to take care of your relationships with others, as the ODD child will exploit any weaknesses in those relationships. And everyone involved in an ODD child's life needs to talk *directly* with each other! The psychiatrist Dr. Jim Chandler (see Further Reading, p.209), amongst his other excellent suggestions given here, implores that we *do not believe what the child with ODD says about others.* ODD kids are masters at assigning blame onto other people. Parents are told incorrect, horrible stories about teachers; fathers about mothers; and vice versa.

- Discuss the need for direct communication in advance of any problems.

- Schedule regular meetings between the school and parents.

- Confirm everything with direct communication.

Another good idea is to limit "screen time." Screen time refers to any activity that has a screen, such as T.V., videogames, computer games, instant messaging, and the Internet. These activities can be clearly addicting, often teach negative behaviors, may agitate the kids, and are difficult to get kids to stop using them. The American Academy of Pediatrics recommends limiting media time to one or two hours per day. It is true, though, that holding screen time as a reward for good behavior can be a powerful tool.

If symptoms are worsening rather than improving, professional help should be sought. Problems are most responsive when interventions begin at an earlier age. Options include:

- professional help for the treatment of co-occurring ADHD, depression, LD, etc.

- family counseling (to improve communication and examine the issue of exposure to violence or abuse)

- parental management training (to help break the downhill spiral of parent/child interactions)

- social skills group training (to learn flexibility and improve the child's tolerance of peers)

- cognitive behavioral therapy (to learn problem solving skills)

- individual psychotherapy.

There is evidence that parental management training for the parents, along with social skills group training for the children, work well together. However, relatively little research has been done on the most effective management techniques. Apparently, researchers avoid ODD children just like other people may do.

## Medication

There are no medications that directly change your "attitude." However, medications are often needed to treat the underlying or comorbid parts of the syndrome mix that are triggering the ODD symptoms. Medication may be used to great effect in the treatment of ADHD, depression, BD, or anxiety disorders.

Medications such as mood stabilizers (eg. Depakote, Lamictal, and Tegretol), atypical neuroleptics (such as Risperdal), and Catapres, can sometimes help with impulsivity and aggression. These are discussed in Chapter 14.

## Chapter 13

# Central Auditory Processing Disorders

Teacher: "Okay, class. Be quiet, go to your seats, take out your math book, open to page 46, and do every other problem starting with question number 3."

Pause. John gets lost after "Be quiet."

Teacher: "John, you haven't even opened your book yet—even though I know you are good at math. You didn't do what I just said to do. Don't you care?"

What happened?

## What is central auditory processing?

When a sound vibration hits our eardrum, a series of small bones transmits the information to nerve receptors located in our inner ear. These receptors send the raw information towards our brain via the auditory nerves. Central auditory processing (CAP), like its name says, is the central nervous system's processing (of that unrefined auditory information coming from our auditory nerves) into something useful. In its simplest terms, CAP is the analysis and interpretation of information from our ears, or "what we do with what the ear hears."

Central auditory processing disorders (CAPD), then, are problems with one or more aspects of the CAP process. CAPD is not a single disease entity, but rather a group of problems that can occur singly or in combination. This group of conditions is sometimes also called APD —auditory processing disorders. CAPD is felt to occur in about 2–3% of the population, with boys outnumbering girls by 2:1 (Schminky and Baran 1999).

So much for the simple answers. Now, let's examine in some more detail the specific processes involved in processing noise once you have detected it. Note that these steps overlap and are inseparable. Do not be thrown off by the fancy terms—they mean just what they say.

- ☐ *Discrimination*—the ability to discriminate the different pitch, duration, and intensity (loudness) of the sounds. This essential hearing task will affect progress in virtually all academic skills.

- ☐ *Auditory discrimination*—the ability to discriminate (distinguish) between words that sound similar to each other, such as between "hip" and "hit." Importantly, background noise makes this process significantly harder for children with CAPD.

- ☐ *Localization*—the ability to determine where a sound is coming from; and, thus, where you should direct you attention.

- ☐ *Auditory attention*—the ability to sustain attention to that sound.

- ☐ *Auditory figure-ground*—the ability to separate out the primary sound (the "figure," such as the teacher's voice) from the background sound (the "ground," such as other noise in the classroom). Imagine your own experience listening to a friend at a noisy party. Imagine if your whole day was like that.

- ☐ *Auditory closure*—the process whereby we can still understand the whole word or message even if part of it is missing or degraded. Our nervous system has a great deal of redundancy built in, and can usually fill in the gaps (i.e., provide "closure"). Again, consider your experience at a noisy party. You can carry on a complete conversation without even hearing much of what the other person is saying.

☐ *Auditory synthesis*—the ability to synthesize/blend isolated phonemes (sounds) into words. An example would be blending the sounds "puh"—"uh"—"te" together to form the word pronounced "put." Clearly, this is an essential step in reading.

☐ *Auditory analysis*—the ability to identify parts of words embedded within the word (for example, help*s* versus help*ed*). In particular, this skill is essential to develop verb tenses.

☐ *Auditory association*—the ability to attach a meaning, once we have isolated and refined the noise into a word or specific sound. Frankly, it is astounding that most of us have the instant ability to know that the sound "h-o-t" means "something that could burn you."

☐ *Auditory memory*—the ability to store and later recall what we have heard.

Other needed skills, but that are not unique to auditory processing, include attention, language, and memory.

All of these CAP steps happen on the sensory (input) side of language—occurring particularly in our brainstem and temporal lobes. This must all occur before we can even get to the other cognitive processes accomplished by the rest of the brain: figuring out the answer to what we just heard, expressing the answer, and acting upon our answer. It is amazing that any of us can communicate at all.

## Diagnosing CAPD
### Symptoms

Given all of the component skills that are encompassed by the initials CAPD, it is not surprising that there is a large shopping list of possible symptoms. The following list includes some of the warning signs to make us *consider* the diagnosis of CAPD, and possibly undertake further testing. Making matters worse, once again, is the high frequency in which CAPD co-occurs, mimics, and worsens other conditions of the syndrome mix covered in this book, such as attention deficit hyperactivity disorder (ADHD) and language problems.

Consider CAPD when a student shows:

- difficulty with hearing in a noisy environment, or over the phone

- difficulty whereby competing noises scramble comprehension (All of us have to work harder to *hear* when the room gets noisy. CAPD kids may have to work harder to *understand* in a noisy room. It is as if the competing noise not only drowns out the teacher's voice, but also turns on an eggbeater and scrambles it.)

- unusual sensitivity or complaints about noise

- difficulty telling the direction from which someone is talking

- difficulty sustaining and directing attention, especially against competing noises

- difficulty following multi-step directions, especially if given in one sentence

- difficulty following long conversations

- difficulty remembering information presented aurally (people with CAPD may prefer viewing videos with the written subtitles turned on)

- confusion over words with similar sounds

- difficulty learning a foreign language or uncommon vocabulary words

- lack of awareness of the speaker

- lack of understanding ("I heard you, but I don't know what you mean")

- difficulty with organization

- non-verbal problems (such as music appreciation)

- verbal IQ (intelligence quotient) lower than performance IQ

- poor performance in auditory based psycho-educational tests

- reading, spelling, or speech problems (if the child does not hear words properly, then all tasks based initially on phonics are at risk)

- unexplained poor academic performance

- hearing loss.

## Distinguishing CAPD from ADHD

It is easy to confuse CAPD and ADHD (especially of the inattentive type) as they can co-occur with each other and share:

- difficulty paying attention

- difficulty telling the foreground from the background noise

- difficulty with following a sequence of directions.

We can note some distinguishing features, though, in Table 13.1.

Table 13.1 Distinguishing features of ADHD and CAPD

| ADHD | CAPD |
|---|---|
| Difficulty attending to all non-intriguing tasks. | Difficulty attending to listening related tasks |
| Background noise makes it harder to attend to the information. | Background noise scrambles the information. |
| Students typically can understand, once you get their attention. | Students may have trouble with comprehension of oral tasks, even once you get their attention. |
| Executive function difficulties. | Executive function relatively intact, as long as the child understands the task at hand. |
| May be physically hyperactive, over-reactive, or impulsive. | Unless acting out from academic frustration, students are not usually disruptive. |
| Typically do not have memory problems. | May have auditory memory problems. |

## Testing

As we can see, the warning symptoms for potential CAPD are quite variable, and some are not very specific. Once the diagnosis is considered, we need further testing—even though that is still not perfect. Full CAPD testing requires specialized equipment, and is typically done by an audiologist or speech therapist with particular training in the area.

Typically, children need to be seven years old before the testing is reliable, although some tests can be done by age five. In addition, results are difficult to interpret in children with low IQ, language problems, or ADHD. CAPD testing is usually done as part of a larger psycho-educational evaluation. The child's clinical symptoms help to guide the choice of tests.

The following descriptions will help you to understand these specialized tests, and to better understand the particular problems that they test for.

- □ *Baseline audiometric peripheral hearing test—"a hearing test."* The first step is to be sure that the child is actually capable of hearing sounds at different frequencies and volumes. A hearing loss does not preclude the possibility of a CAPD, but certainly makes testing for it more difficult.

- □ *Brainstem auditory evoked responses (BAER).* This test is like a mini-EEG (electroencephalogram). Sounds are played into earphones, which evoke responses from the child's nervous system. Electrodes are placed on the child's head to check for any delay of these electrical impulses as they work their way through the brainstem and the rest of the brain.

- □ *Monaural low redundancy speech tests.* In these tests, the sounds are presented "monaurally," i.e., to one ear at a time. The sounds are degraded—by cutting out part of the sounds electronically, changing their frequency, etc. This lowers the normal redundancy that we depend upon to figure out the word. These tests stress the system, and check how well the student can figure out and complete sounds ("auditory closure").

□ *Dichotic speech tests.* Here, sounds are presented to both ears, either simultaneously or in an overlapping manner. The child repeats the words. He may be asked to say everything he heard, which tests his listening even when his attention is divided among multiple sources ("divided attention"). Or he may have to say only what he heard from one ear, which tests how well he can direct his attention ("directed attention").

□ *Temporal patterning tests.* The ability to process non-verbal sounds is tested in this group of tests. For example, the child may be asked to hum a pattern of sounds that she heard, or to describe the pattern.

□ *Binaural integration/interaction tests.* Different parts of the speech signal are presented to different ears, and the child's ability to integrate those signals into a single sound is tested. For example, a "d" sound is played into the right ear while an "og" sound is played into the left ear. A typical child would have no difficulty blending these sounds into "dog."

## Treatments at home and school

There is no single set of recommendations that applies to this diverse group of difficulties. A specific plan needs to be made for the set of deficits diagnosed in each child. Treatments include modifying the environment, working directly on the deficit, and circumventing the deficit. Many of the following suggestions come from an excellent Technical Assistance Paper from the Florida Department of Education (2001).

Ensure appropriate seating:

- Seat the child near the action. Preferably, place the student three to four feet from the main action, but up to six to eight feet away is okay. This will allow the child to maximize visual and audio cues, as well as help with attention. As the focus of the class moves, the child may need to move as well. However, we also need to:

- Avoid competing noises! As we have seen, background noises can scramble the signal for CAPD children. Avoid doorways, noisy window areas, bubbling fish tanks, humming lights, nearby bathrooms, etc.

- Provide a quiet, private study area if needed—both in school and at home.

- Provide mufflers/ear plugs if needed. In order to minimize any stigma, allow other children to use mufflers as well.

Get and keep the child's attention:

- Get the child's visual and auditory attention. This will allow for maximal use of multisensory learning, which is essential for students who have problems with information coming through one sense.

- Establish eye contact when speaking (unless this is uncomfortable for the child). At home, turn off the television; and be sure that you are in the same room as the child while you are talking.

- Cue the children with directives such as "THIS IS IMPORTANT!" or "Remember this!"

- Mark transition periods clearly with appropriate advance warnings and directions for the new task.

- Use predictable daily routines.

- Provide help with note taking. It may be difficult to pay attention to the teacher, the teacher's voice, and take notes all at the same time.

- Attention issues may be worse at school due to the commotion. However, they may be worse at home because who can maintain so much effort all day long? Don't blame the child if he listens better at school or at home.

When talking to the child:

- Speak clearly, slowly, and with comfortable loudness.

- Vary your tone of voice and rate of speech to keep attention and emphasize important material.

- Use natural gestures that support your words, but are not so excessive that they distract the child.

- Give direct and uncomplicated directions.

- Give directions one at a time, in order.

- Allow time to process each direction.

- Repeat directions as needed, preferably using simpler language.

- Model/demonstrate the directions if possible. Teachers can write directions as they say them. Write a list of the steps.

- Don't assume that the child understands the subtle parts of your comments.

- Encourage the student to ask for clarification, if needed. Never say, "What, weren't you listening?"

- Check the child's comprehension by asking her to repeat what she heard using different words.

- Check that the child understands by monitoring her progress frequently—making sure that the work is being done as directed. This will help avoid the deflating experience of doing a great job at the wrong task.

- Look for "avoidance," which may really be a lack of comprehension.

- A low teacher–student ratio may be helpful.

- A student peer may help explain material.

Teachers, parents, and the child can all share with each other their insights into how the child learns best.

Use the tactics of preview and review:

- Review old material before presenting something new.

- Preview new material before the primary presentation. This can be via a brief summary of the new material, or by providing material to review at home before coming to class.

- Show how the information relates to the child's life.

- Write an outline on the board, along with new vocabulary.

- Frequently summarize key points, and ask students for summaries.

- CAPD students may benefit from individualized help.

Facilitate time management:

- Allow extra time—for tests and for individual classroom responses.

- Break up academic activity to avoid fatigue.

- Schedule the most intense academics in the morning, for most students.

- Encourage the use of an assignment book and organizer. Monitor its use!

Teach compensatory techniques:

- Encourage the child to use multisensory learning—such as saying, writing, and visualizing the material to be learned. Some children benefit from pretending to write the material in the air.

- Allow the child to subvocalize, if needed.

- Teach how to use mnemonics. For example, we learned how to read music notes on the staff by the mnemonic "F-A-C-E."

- Teach how to use "visual grids" as hooks from which to hang information. For example, on the left side of the grid are the points in favor of the Democrats, and on the right side are the points in favor of the Republicans. If a child simply remembers which side of the page he saw the fact on, he can assign it to the correct political party. These grids can be written on paper, and later recalled visually to help sort out the information.

- Teach how to chunk information into small sections, to facilitate memory. For example, rather than remembering six random American history events, divide them into those occurring before the American Revolution and those after.

Rather than remembering 243564875, remember 243 564 875.

- Teach how to use spellcheck.

- Some children might benefit from material being recorded; but, honestly, who has time to listen to the whole day again?

Classroom adaptations can often help:

- FM (frequency modulated) amplifiers may be suggested by the audiologist. They are useful for those subtypes of CAPD marked by inability to separate the foreground from the background noise, difficulty integrating material, or difficulty organizing information. The system is basically a closed-circuit radio set up. The teacher wears a microphone, and the student wears an earphone. This amplifies the teacher's voice, making it easier to distinguish it from background noise. But many students will not tolerate the "stigma" attached with such a system.

- Improve classroom acoustics with drapes, carpet, and sound-absorbing wall hangings and bulletin boards. Tennis balls placed under chair legs will reduce noise.

- Arrange the classroom to allow individual and small group settings.

- Avoid open classrooms.

*Chapter 14*

# Medications[1]

## Medicating kids? What is this world coming to?

Before we can discuss the individual medications, we need to address a more basic question: Is it ethical to give psychoactive medications to children?

Let's begin with a brief survey, to clarify what group of children we are discussing. Raise your hand if you are in favor of the following:

1. A child who has no problem ➔ gets no medicine. (I assume we are all raising our hands. Certainly, I am.)

2. A child who has a problem that can be handled without medication ➔ gets no medication. (Again, I assume we are all raising our hands.) Now, for the big question.

3. A child who has a neurologically based problem, and behavioral interventions have been unable to preserve the child's happiness ➔ gets medication to see if it can help. (I hope that, given these qualifications, we are raising our hands as well.)

---

1   Disclaimer: This information is not intended to be all-inclusive and does not constitute medical advice. It is not a substitute for discussion between patients and their doctors. Like most areas of information, knowledge about mental health issues and medication is likely to change over time. Medication updates can be found at www.FDA.gov. Some of the common medication uses described in this text are not yet US FDA approved.

When a child is brought to my medical office, it is almost never the first step. Enticements, bribes, threats, pretending that it will soon go away, and prayer have been tried first. It is great if those interventions are successful. However, if they have not succeeded in preserving the child's self-esteem, then I invoke the following basic strategy: "*If it's working, keep doing it. If it's not, do something else.*" Sometimes, that something else is medication.

## Benefits of medication

In the bad old days, there was little distinction between epilepsy, migraines (with their weird vision attacks followed by dropping to the floor in pain), psychiatric disease, and witchcraft. Mercifully, the Dark Age concepts of epilepsy and migraines have been largely dropped in modern times. Most of us do not think of people with epilepsy as being possessed, or weak of spirit. It's brain biochemistry. We don't tell them to "Just get your act together!" It currently makes perfect sense to use anticonvulsants for seizures, just like it makes sense to use insulin for diabetes when diet does not work.

Unfortunately, many of us are still a few centuries behind when it comes to psychiatric disease. MRI (magnetic resonance imaging) scans, PET (positron emission tomography) scans, adoption studies, and more, show the biochemical basis of much of psychiatric disease. When behavioral and environmental interventions do not work, then it makes sense to use biochemical interventions, i.e. medications for biochemical problems.

People with attention deficit hyperactivity disorder (ADHD), obsessive-compulsive disorder (OCD), bipolar depression (BD), Tourette's syndrome, etc. did not ask to have their problems. It has nothing to do with lack of will power.

### WHAT IF THEY DISCOVER SOMETHING BAD ABOUT THESE DRUGS?

No one can guarantee that, fifty years from now, there might not be some side-effect that we do not know about currently. Many of these medications already do have a long safety record, such as stimulants that have been used for 40 years. Other medications have quite limited experience in children. When possible, we use the safest medication with the longest safety record. We try to navigate the best course. There are no guarantees in life. Life has risks.

For some children, though, there is a risk associated with *not* using medication. There are often huge difficulties for these children if we cannot help them get on the right track—problems with poor school performance, unhappiness, and substance abuse. By the time these children are being considered for medication, they are often well on the road to these risks—and getting deeper into these problems.

So when we talk about the possible risks of medication, it needs to be weighed against the risks of no medication. For some children, the known immediate risk of their condition outweighs a possible unknown medical one.

### DON'T THESE DRUGS LEAD TO SUBSTANCE ABUSE?

Many people fear that the use of psychoactive drugs in children will lead to future substance abuse. Actually, all of the evidence points to the opposite. Multiple studies have shown that stimulant treatment for ADHD cuts the risk of future substance abuse by more than half (e.g., Wilens *et al.* 2003). In other words, there is a huge *protective effect* of stimulants against substance abuse. Research has not been done yet to show why stimulants lower the risk of substance abuse in ADHD people; but presumably, those people who are now able to find success in society have less need to seek alternate forms of pleasure or escape. It is actually fair to ask, "How can we withhold a treatment, when withholding the treatment doubles the child's risk for substance abuse?"

### HOW WILL PEOPLE EVER LEARN TO HANDLE THEIR OWN PROBLEMS IF THEY RELY ON MEDICATION?

Once again, medications are to be added after attempts to get the child to "handle" his own problem have already failed, or to make those interventions more likely to succeed. The medications give the child the basic tools that they need to comply with behavioral approaches. For example, once you have given a child a reasonable attention span, then we can ask him to behave in class.

"But aren't we being too soft on these kids?" No! They are already having a tough life, and even on medication, their life will still be tougher than typical. By the time medication is prescribed, the person will have already been struggling with these issues far more than typical people. The medications are not perfect. The difficulty will continue, but it will now be a tolerable and fair fight. There will still be plenty of opportunity to build character.

## Attitudes to medications

Let's not confuse being "famous" with being "infamous." Drugs such as Ritalin and Prozac have garnered a lot of press. Many people think that "famous" must mean "bad." We should remember, though, that drugs usually only make it to the front cover of a magazine because they are used frequently. In turn, they are only used frequently because they are they are effective and relatively safe. Just because you have heard about a medication does not mean that it is a bad medication.

### WHO MAKES THE DECISION TO USE MEDICATIONS?

Ultimately, the choice to use medication is made by the family, the child, and the physician. We depend—often quite significantly—upon data from a multitude of sources, including the school. Teachers and other school professionals are our eyes and ears. However, medical decisions are made between the child's family and doctor.

Doctors also depend upon the frontline observers to let us know if and when the medication is working; and if and when side-effects are seen.

### INTERNATIONAL DIFFERENCES

Clearly, different medications are used with different frequency in different countries. This probably has more to do with different diagnostic criteria, societal views on medication, and societal expectations than with actual differences in rates of the disorders.

The brand names and the indications for drug usage contained in this book are given from a U.S. common practice perspective. Note that the pediatric use of some of these medications has not been formally approved by the U.S. Food and Drug Administration.

This information does not constitute medical advice, which can only be obtained on an individualized basis by a properly licensed physician or other professional.

## Medications for ADHD

### Stimulants: An overview

The medications commonly referred to as "stimulants" have the longest and probably best track record in treating ADHD. They increase levels of the brain transmitters dopamine and norepinephrine. This wakes up the frontal lobes, so that they can now do a better job at executive functions such as inhibiting distractions and impulsivity.

To refresh our memory about the bicycle analogy, ADHDers are like bicycles without brakes. They careen around, unable to go anywhere but where gravity takes them. The stimulants are analogous to waking up the bicycle's brake linings. Stimulants are *not* like sedatives. Sedatives would be analogous to pouring tar on the bike's gears—making the child too tired to bother anyone. That would be a horrible thing to do. Stimulants, again, are just the opposite. They make a higher-performing bike.

There is nothing paradoxical about stimulants having a "calming" effect in children or adults. In a person of any age, they function the same: the person sits still because they are now properly awake, not because they are sedated. It works in the same fashion as adults who take coffee.

#### METHYLPHENIDATE PREPARATIONS (SHORT-ACTING)

- ☐ **Ritalin** contains the gold standard of stimulants—methylphenidate, the generic name of the active chemical in Ritalin. Ritalin tablets last only about two to five hours. Thus, Ritalin required frequent dosing, including the infamous trip to the school nurse at lunchtime. Even the lunch dose of Ritalin wore out by homework time, leading to frequent fights with parents over homework. Rebound—a period of nasty, irrational behavior occurring as the medication level drops rapidly—has been most common with the short-acting preparations.

- ☐ **Focalin (d-methylphenidate)** is just the active part of methylphenidate (just the d-isomer). It seems to last a little longer than regular Ritalin, and requires only half of the dose.

#### METHYLPHENIDATE PREPARATIONS (LONG-ACTING)

Long-lasting preparations of methylphenidate are replacing traditional short-acting forms. Although swallowed once in the morning, these formulations keep releasing the medication throughout the day. This saves children from going to the nurse at lunchtime, and some preparations last long enough to allow more children to benefit from medication effect during homework time—a practice that is clearly recommended. In addition, these preparations seem to have less rebound (irritability that some kids get when the medicine wears off).

□ **Concerta**. Concerta was the first good long-acting preparation of methylphenidate to be marketed. It approximates the release of three doses of methylphenidate, giving it an effective life of about 10+ hours. The first dose is contained in the outer coating of the capsule, and is released within the first hour. Inside the capsule is a sponge, which absorbs fluid from the gastrointestinal tract. The expanding sponge then slowly pushes two separate doses of medication out of the other end of the capsule. Concerta is designed to release a higher proportion of medication later in the day.

□ **Metadate CD**. This capsule uses beads that release their methyl-phenidate at different times, to approximate a twice a day dosage. Metadate CD is designed to release more of its medication earlier in the day. The capsules can be opened and sprinkled on applesauce.

□ **Ritalin LA**. This capsule functions similarly to Metadate CD. It is an effective preparation should not be confused with the older Ritalin SR, which is the previous, less effective wax matrix release formula-tion. The Ritalin LA capsules can be opened and sprinkled on applesauce.

### DEXTRO-AMPHETAMINE PREPARATIONS

□ **Dexedrine tablets** (with a four-hour effect) and **Dexedrine span-sules** (with a 10-hour effect) are the brand names for dextro-amphet-amine preparations.

### MIXED AMPHETAMINE SALT PREPARATIONS

□ **Adderall tablets** (with a four to six-hour effect) and **Adderall XR spansules** (with a 10+ hour effect) have become common choices in the treatment of ADHD—especially the XR form. Adderall is a mixture of different kinds of dexto- and levo-amphetamine. The capsules can be opened and sprinkled on applesauce. There is also a generic form of Adderall tablets. According to the recently revised package insert, "Sudden death has been reported in association with amphetamine treatment at usual doses in children with structural cardiac abnormalities. Adderall XR generally should not be used in children or adults with structural cardiac abnormailities." (Package insert 2005) Updates on this issue can be found on the U.S. Food and Drug Administration's website at www.FDA.gov.

### CYLERT (PEMOLINE)

☐ **Cylert** (the brand name for pemoline) is rarely started any more due to possible rare liver toxicity.

## Which stimulant to use?

As of this writing, there is no data or consensus as to the best stimulant preparation. Most experts would agree, though, that:

- the long-lasting preparations are preferable to the short-acting ones

- if one class of stimulants does not work, or causes side-effects, then trial with another preparation should be considered

- if a long-lasting preparation still does not last long enough, than a short-acting preparation can be added at the end of the afternoon

- most children benefit from the use of medication during homework time; and if medication allows the child to get better feedback on weekends, then it can be used at those times as well.

### POSSIBLE SIDE-EFFECTS OF STIMULANTS

Considering how effective they can be, the stimulants are usually quite well tolerated. Most children "feel nothing" when they take it. Observant students notice that they get their work done more efficiently; and, for some reason, people seem to yell at them less. However, they don't feel anything, any more than people "feel" anything when they wear their glasses. Normalcy has no feeling.

There are possible side-effects, though:

- Loss of appetite (particularly for lunch) is the most common issue, but occurs in only a fraction of kids—about 4% of patients, according to the Concerta package insert.

- Insomnia is the other most common issue, but again occurs in only a fraction of children—about 4% of patients, according to the Concerta package insert—and tends to improve over time.

- Headache.

- Tics can be worsened, unchanged, or improved by stimulants.

- Stimulants do not seem to "stunt your growth." Any possible mild height difference in ADHD kids appears to be due to the ADHD itself, not the medication used to treat it.

- Multiples studies show that stimulants as prescribed do not increase the risk of substance abuse, and in fact, lower the risk (e.g., Wilens *et al.* 2003).

- Stimulants may provoke mania in people who are already prone to it or possibly worsen other behaviors.

- Stimulants are extremely unlikely to cause systemic problems such as heart, liver or bone marrow. See cardiac warnings under Adderall.

## Non-stimulants for ADHD

☐ **Strattera** (atomoxetine is the generic name) was released in late 2002. Unlike the stimulants, Strattera has direct effect only upon the neurotransmitter norepinephrine. In other words, it has no direct dopaminergic effect. As such, it seems to be less of a risk for worsening tics, anxiety, or mood disorders (or insomnia in children). It can still cause decreased appetite; and unlike stimulants, can frequently be sedating when started. Its full effect may not be observed for several weeks. There have been recent reports about liver problems with

Strattera—a situation that will need clarification. Follow updates at www.FDA.gov. The exact place for this new medication in the treatment of ADHD is not fully defined as of this writing.

☐ **Catapres** (clonidine) and **Tenex** (guanfacine) are "alpha 2 agonists" which increase frontal lobe function. These medications seem to be most useful for impulsivity (as opposed to inattention). They are also utilized in the treatment of tics, and so are used frequently in Tourette's syndrome when tics and ADHD co-occur. Clonidine's sedating effects are minimized by the use of small frequent doses of the tablet form, or of a skin patch preparation. Although also used as anti-hypertensive medications, they rarely cause any significant cardiovascular effects in our children. The school nurse may be asked to occasionally monitor the child's blood pressure.

☐ **Other medications** for ADHD include Wellbutrin (bupropion) and tricyclic antidepressants (see section below on depression).

## Medications for depression

Current research attributes biochemical depression to insufficient release by the brainstem of two neurotransmitters onto the cortex: serotonin and norepinephrine. Pharmacological treatments are thus aimed at raising the levels of these transmitters. The mainstays of antidepressants are the selective serotonin reuptake inhibitors (SSRIs).

*As of this writing, there is concern regarding the possible relationship of all antidepressants to increasing suicidal thoughts.* This concern includes, but is not limited to, the SSRIs; and exists even if the "antidepressants" are being used for indications other than depression, such as for anxiety. The periods of presumed greatest risk are with starting, increasing, or tapering of the medications. It is fair to say that more research will be helpful; and that any child, whether on antidepressant medication or not, should be carefully monitored for ideation of self-harm. Updates can be found at www.FDA.gov.

## SSRIs

Selective serotonin reuptake inhibitor (SSRI) medications selectively increases brain levels of serotonin by blocking its removal from the synapse. More serotonin. Less depression. Other drugs in the past have increased serotonin levels, but have not been selective about it, i.e., have raised other transmitter levels as well. Those undesirable transmitter levels have caused undesirable side-effects.

The big fuss about SSRIs, then, is that their selectivity allows us to use highly effective doses on serotonin levels with fewer unpleasant side-effects from other neurotransmitters. The SSRIs are usually medically quite safe, but some people may experience some unwelcome side-effects.

The most common SSRI side-effects are:

- weight gain

- sedation or insomnia

- sexual dysfunction

- occasional "dysinhibition," when the child gets more activated or agitated

- provocation of mania in people who are prone to it.

SSRIs may take up to four to six weeks to become effective, unlike the stimulants that work immediately.

☐ **Prozac** (fluoxetine): Prozac has been proven to help depression in about two thirds of children. This is the only antidepressant that actually has approval for use in pediatric depression from the U.S. Food and Drug Administration. The doctor, though, may recommend other antidepressants. Other SSRIs include:

☐ **Luvox** (fluvoxamine)—the brand "Luvox" is no longer manufactured

☐ **Zoloft** (sertraline)

☐ **Paxil** (paroxetine)

□ **Celexa** (citalopram)

□ **Lexapro** (the active half of citalopram).

## Other antidepressants

□ **Wellbutrin** (bupropion) has been used with some apparent success for childhood depression as well as ADHD.

□ **Effexor** (venlafaxine) is not currently recommended for use in children.

□ **Elavil** (amitriptyline) and other traditional tricyclic antidepressants have been shown to be ineffective for depression in children and adolescents.

## Medications for anxiety

Regardless of the reason for their use, as of this writing, there is controversy regarding the possible relationship of any antidepressant in suicidal thoughts. See above. This warning would apply to the use of antidepressants in children who are even being treated with antidepressants for reasons other than depression—such as for anxiety or OCD.

## SSRIs

SSRIs are again the mainstay of medical treatment for anxiety, providing moderate to marked improvement in four out of five children with anxiety disorder.

## Other medications

### TRICYCLIC ANTIDEPRESSANT MEDICATIONS

Tricyclic medications are very effective for panic attacks, and many of them are quite helpful for anxiety in general. Their name derives from a chemical structure with three cyclic rings, hence "tricyclic."

The tricyclic medications tend to increase levels of multiple neurotransmitters (in contrast to the "selective" serotonin reuptake inhibitors.) The tricyclics increase levels of serotonin and norepinephrine, but also affect histamine and cholinergic receptors.

The common side-effects of the tricyclics are:

- sedation (a frequently significant problem)
- light-headedness
- dry mouth
- constipation
- urinary retention
- rare cardiac effects which have tempered their use, and may require monitoring with electrocariograms (EKGs).

Current tricyclic medications include:

☐ **Pamelor** (nortriptyline)

☐ **Tofranil** (imipramine)

☐ **Elavil** (amitriptyline).

### BENZODIAZEPINE ANTI-ANXIETY MEDICATIONS

The benzodiazepines raise levels of the transmitter GABA (gamma-aminobutyric acid). Although these medications have few serious systemic effects, they tend to be sedating, and require increasing doses over time. The potential exists for dependency on these medications. They are best used for just a short term, while waiting for the other medications to take effect. Like many other psychoactive medications, when they are no longer needed, their dose is typically slowly tapered. Commonly used benzodiazepines include:

☐ **Valium** (diazepam)

☐ **Klonopin** (clonazepam)

☐ **Ativan** (lorazepam)

☐ **Xanax** (alprazolam), which has a particularly short time of effectiveness, leading to frequent problematic rebound anxiety.

### BUSPAR (BUSPIRONE)

Buspar is effective for anxiety but not panic attacks. There are few serious medical side-effects. It is not used as commonly as the SSRIs.

## Medications for OCD

SSRIs are the mainstay of medical treatment for OCD. Zoloft, Prozac, and Luvox all have been currently approved for treatment of OCD in children in the U.S. Studies suggest that some other SSRIs are also effective. Overall, there appears to be a 40% reduction of symptoms (Freeman, J.B. *et al.* 2004). See important information about the SSRIs in the section on depression.

## Medications for bipolar depression

Medications to treat mood instability are called "mood stabilizers." Although there is a great deal of childhood experience with many of these medications for other conditions, their effectiveness in childhood bipolar depression remains poorly tested.

## Anticonvulsants

Anticonvulsants are commonly used as mood stabilizers. These medications may require blood tests for drug levels, complete blood count, and liver function. In general, they are well tolerated. They can cause:

- sedation
- weight gain (particularly Depakote)
- rare effects on the bone marrow or liver (less with Trileptal)
- allergic reactions of the skin, eye, or mouth can be severe.

Anticonvulsants commonly used in bipolar depression include:

☐ **Trileptal** (oxcarbazepine)

☐ **Tegretol** (carbamazepine)

☐ **Depakote** (sodium valproate)

☐ **Lamictal** (lamotrigine).

## Lithium

☐ **Lithium** does not seem to be particularly effective in children, who cycle rapidly between mania and depression.

## Neuroleptics

Neuroleptics are useful in bipolar depression as well, especially for the psychotic and aggressive symptoms. Common neuroleptics include:

☐ **Risperdal** (risperidone)

☐ **Abilify** (aripiprazole)

☐ **Zyprexa** (olanzepine)

☐ **Haldol** (haloperidal)—no longer manufactured under the trade name Haldol

☐ **Orap** (pimozide)—used less commonly because of drug interactions and cardiac effects.

Risperdal, Abilify, and Zyprexa are examples of "atypical neuroleptics" because they have fewer side-effects than the older neuroleptics such as Haldol and Orap. Regardless, there are still significant possible side-effects of this powerful class of medications, such as:

• weight gain

• sedation

• cardiac effects, which are not commonly significant

• a rare movement disorder called "tardive dyskinesia," which is particularly rare in children with the newer atypical neuroleptics

- a rare metabolic condition of high fever, muscle destruction, and confusion called "malignant neuroleptic syndrome"
- possible effects on sugar metabolism
- possible effects on the hormone prolactin.

## Medications for tic disorders

Catapres (clonidine) may frequently be tried first (see p.197), but neuroleptics are usually more effective, though with more potential risks.

# Behavioral Checklist

Child's Name:                 Your Name:

Date:                          Subject (if teacher):

Please rate the severity of each problem listed, and add comments in the margins as needed.

0 = none    1 = slight    2 = moderate    3 = major

|  | 0 | 1 | 2 | 3 |
|---|---|---|---|---|
| Easily distracted | ☐ | ☐ | ☐ | ☐ |
| Requires one-to-one attention to get work done | ☐ | ☐ | ☐ | ☐ |
| Impulsive (trouble waiting turn, blurts out answers) | ☐ | ☐ | ☐ | ☐ |
| Hyperactive (fidgety, trouble staying seated) | ☐ | ☐ | ☐ | ☐ |
| Disorganized | ☐ | ☐ | ☐ | ☐ |
| Does not write down assignments | ☐ | ☐ | ☐ | ☐ |
| Backpack is a mess | ☐ | ☐ | ☐ | ☐ |
| Poor sense of time | ☐ | ☐ | ☐ | ☐ |
| Over-reacts | ☐ | ☐ | ☐ | ☐ |
| Easily overwhelmed | ☐ | ☐ | ☐ | ☐ |
| Blows up easily | ☐ | ☐ | ☐ | ☐ |
| Trouble switching activities | ☐ | ☐ | ☐ | ☐ |
| Poor handwriting | ☐ | ☐ | ☐ | ☐ |

|  | 0 | 1 | 2 | 3 |
|---|---|---|---|---|
| Certain academic tasks seem difficult (specify) | ☐ | ☐ | ☐ | ☐ |
| Anxious, edgy, stressed or painfully worried | ☐ | ☐ | ☐ | ☐ |
| Obsessive thoughts or fears; perseverative rituals | ☐ | ☐ | ☐ | ☐ |
| Seems *deliberately* spiteful, cruel or annoying | ☐ | ☐ | ☐ | ☐ |
| Irritated for hours or days on end (not just frequent, brief blow-ups) | ☐ | ☐ | ☐ | ☐ |
| Depressed, "empty," sad, or unhappy | ☐ | ☐ | ☐ | ☐ |
| Extensive mood swings | ☐ | ☐ | ☐ | ☐ |
| Tics: repetitive movements or noises | ☐ | ☐ | ☐ | ☐ |
| Poor eye contact | ☐ | ☐ | ☐ | ☐ |
| Does not catch on to social cues | ☐ | ☐ | ☐ | ☐ |
| Limited range of interests and interactions | ☐ | ☐ | ☐ | ☐ |
| Unusual sensitivity to sounds, touch, textures, movement, or taste | ☐ | ☐ | ☐ | ☐ |
| Coordination difficulties | ☐ | ☐ | ☐ | ☐ |
| Other (specify) | ☐ | ☐ | ☐ | ☐ |

If the child is on medication, please answer the following questions:

Can you tell when the child is on medication or not?

Does the medication work consistently throughout the day?

Does the child appear to be on too much or too little medication?

Other comments:

# Quick Quiz on Executive Function

Answer the questions below based on the following scenario.

> *John is a bright, college-bound 8th grade student with ADHD (attention deficit hyperactivity disorder). He does not write down a required essay into his assignment pad, and does not hand in the required work. His teacher tells him that if John simply hands in the essay tomorrow, then it will still receive full credit.*
>
> *This time, the teacher watches John write down the assignment on a slip of paper. John thanks the teacher, truly intends to do it, walks into the hall and throws the slip into his backpack. When he arrives home, his mother asks him about his homework, but the subject of the essay never comes up. John never does hand it in. The teacher gives John a zero, hoping that it will teach him a lesson for next time.*

1. John primarily hurts himself by this behavior.

    (a) True

    (b) False

2. There are logical reasons why people would choose to "shoot themselves in their own foot."

    (a) True

    (b) False

3. Instead, problems with executive function could explain this behavior.

    (a) True

    (b) False

4. Organization problems are common in ADHD.

    (a)  True

    (b)  False

5. John comes home, finds the note, and yet never tells his mother. This can be best explained by:

    (a)  John is lazy, and yet somehow musters enough energy to deliberately sabotage his own future.

    (b)  John wants to deceive his mother, even though he has been granted "amnesty" if he just hands it in.

    (c)  John lives in the next four seconds. For the next four seconds, the most appealing choice is to ignore the problem.

6. This teacher has already gone above and beyond typical understanding and guidance.

    (a)  True

    (b)  False

7. The purpose of giving John a "zero" is to:

    (a)  Cause him to squirm.

    (b)  Alter his behavior next time.

8. For people with ADHD, there is no "next time."

    (a)  True

    (b)  False

9. Giving John a "zero" is likely to alter his ADHD behavior next time.

    (a)  True

    (b)  False

10. If a strategy doesn't work, it makes sense to:

    (a)  Keep repeating it, hoping the 53rd time will be the charm.

    (b)  Try something else.

11. The reason why John doesn't act like everyone else is that:

    (a)  He *can't* consistently act like everyone else.

    (b)  He likes getting yelled at.

12. Entrusting a child who has executive function problems with his own organization and future planning is a good idea.

   (a) True

   (b) False

13. Direct communication between the teacher and the parent or skills teacher is more likely to be a successful intervention.

   (a) True

   (b) False

14. Most children shouldn't need this type of continuous support. It's "weird" that John does. That is why he has a diagnosable condition.

   (a) True

   (b) False

15. This all makes sense during this quiz. The next time I encounter such a situation in the real world, I will...

**Answers should be self-evident.**

# Further Reading
## Books and Internet Resources

### General neurobehavioral information
### Books

Pliszka, S., Carlson, C., and Swanson, J. (2001) *ADHD with Comorbid Disorders*. New York: Guilford Press. Presents an encyclopedic review of the literature on drug and behavioral treatments. Intended for professional use.

Ratey, J. and Johnson, C. (1998) *Shadow Syndromes*. New York: Bantam Books. This book explains that many symptoms such as attention deficit hyperactivity disorder (ADHD), obsessions, rage, autism, etc. can occur at "subsyndromal" levels. Human brains are not "all or nothing."

Shore, K. (2002) *Special Kids Problem Solver: Ready-to-Use Interventions for Helping All Students with Academic, Behavioral and Physical Problems*. San Francisco: Jossey-Bass. The title is says it all.

Wiener, J.M. and Dulcan, M.K. (eds) (2004) *Textbook of Child and Adolescent Psychiatry*, 3rd edition. Arlington, VA: American Psychiatric Publishing. This is a professional level textbook.

### Internet resources

*www.PediatricNeurology.com* is the author's website, featuring detailed information and links on most of the conditions covered in this book, as well as other pediatric neurological issues such as headaches and seizures.

Pediatric Psychiatry Pamphlets at *www.klis.com/chandler/home.htm* by Dr. Jim Chandler provide good natured, accessible, concise, responsible information on a large variety of conditions including ADHD, oppositional defiant disorder (ODD), obsessive-compulsive disorder (OCD), tics, panic, and bipolar disorders.

*www.NeuroPsychologyCentral.com* has excellent links on neuropsychology topics.

Mental health links at *www.baltimorepsych.com/consumer.htm* has topics succinctly covered as part of a great psychiatry site produced by Northern County Psychiatric Associates.

*www.ADDwarehouse.com* carries a full selection of books for teachers and parents on the whole spectrum of neurobehavioral disorders, not just ADHD.

*www.FDA.gov* posts updates on medication emanating from the U.S. Food and Drug Administration.

## Attention deficit hyperactivity disorder (ADHD)
## Books

Barkley, R. (1997) *ADHD and the Nature of Self Control.* New York: Guilford Press. More on the theory of ADHD, with some excellent practical advice. Fairly advanced reading.

Barkley, R. (1998) *Attention-Deficit Hyperactive Disorder: A Handbook for Diagnosis and Treatment, 2nd edition.* New York: Guilford Press. The scientific and unbelievably extensive literature review of ADHD underlying Dr. Barkley's concepts. Like most medical "handbooks," it barely fits in your hand. Quite advanced reading.

Barkley, R. (2000) *Taking Charge of ADHD.* New York: Guilford Press. Dr. Barkley offers ground-breaking material on the nature of ADHD and executive functions. Harder, less optimistic reading.

Green, C., and Chee, K. (1997) *Understanding ADHD.* New York: Vermilion. This book addresses serious issues in an upbeat, even funny, style. A great place to start reading.

Hallowell, E.M., and Ratey, J.R. (1995) *Driven to Distraction.* New York: Simon and Schuster. This excellent book about ADHD has become the standard starting point, especially for adults with ADHD. Many parents might find themselves in this book.

Kutscher, M.L. (2003) *ADHD Book: Living Right Now!* White Plains, NY: Neurology Press. The author's complete, succinct book on the extended range of ADHD problems and treatments. Realistic but upbeat.

Phelan, T.W. (1994) *Surviving Your Adolescents: How to Manage and Let Go of Your 13–18 Year Olds.* Glen Ellyn, IL: Child Management Press. Particularly useful for ADHD adolescents, who have a double dose of foresight blindness. Especially encouraging for ADHDer parents, because this book describes how many families of typical teenagers experience difficulty similar to their ADHD teen—and most of them seem to turn into normal adults.

Phelan, T.W. (2000) *All about Attention Deficit Disorder.* Glen Ellyn, IL: Child Management Press. All about ADHD for parents and teachers. Like all of his excellent books on childhood behavior, this book is both very useful and actually fun to read.

Phelan, T.W. (2003) *1-2-3 Magic: Effective Discipline for Children 2–12.* Glen Ellyn, IL: Child Management Press. Not about ADHD per se, but is an excellent way to learn about the "Act, don't yak!" principle of discipline for younger children.

Silver, L. (1999) *Dr. Larry Silver's Advice to Parents with ADHD.* New York: Random House. This text is particularly for ADHD and associated learning disabilities. Easy reading.

Zeigler Dendy, C.A. (1995) *Teenagers with ADD: A Parents' Guide.* Bethesda, MD: Woodbine House. Optimistic and practical advice for teenagers and others with ADHD. It features extensive sections on specific problems such as waking up and organization. There are also extensive lists of school (and home) accommodations.

## Internet resources

CHADD (Children and Adults with Attention Deficit Disorders) at *www.chadd.org* is an excellent, all-inclusive support group with local chapters. Phone: (001) 800-233-4050.

Mental Health Sanctuary at *www.mhsanctuary.com* has excellent links. In particular, see the Resource Page.

National Institutes of Health On-line booklet on ADHD at *www.nimh.nih.gov/publicat/adhd.cfm.*

*www.ADDvance.com* specializes particularly in girls and women with ADHD. They offer a wide range of excellent books. In particular, see their books *Understanding Girls with ADHD* and *Putting on the Brakes.*

*ADDitude Magazine* at *www.additudemag.com* is an electronic version of their excellent print magazine on ADHD.

ADDed Support at *http://groups.msn.com/ADDedSupport/* is an active parent-to-parent message board.

*www.ConductDisorders.com* is another excellent parent-to-parent message board.

*Behavioral Treatment for ADHD: An Overview* by Dr. David Rabiner at *www.athealth.com/Consumer/farticles/Rabiner.html.*

*Attention Deficits: What Teachers Should Know* at *www.dbpeds.org/articles/detail.cfm?id=31.*

Links on developing an IEP (Individual Educational Plan) at
*www.teach-nology.com/teachers/special_ed/iep/*.

Teens with ADHD site and book by Chris Dendy at *www.chrisdendy.com*.

## Internet email newsletters (excellent for reminding yourself of ADHD principles of care)

*www.ADDchoices.com* offers a newsletter for practical information on the spectrum of ADHD behaviors and problems.

*www.ADHDnews.com* is an empathically maintained and useful newsletter on ADHD!

*www.helpforADD.com* by Dr. David Rabiner is a very useful and scientifically sound email newsletter.

*www.ADDresource.com* provides an ADHD newsletter and extensive source of further links.

Stormwatch Newsletter at *www.adhdstormwatch.com* has an upbeat monthly newsletter on ADHD.

## Learning disabilities (LD)
## Books

Osman, B.B. (1997) *Learning Disabilities and ADHD: A Family Guide to Living and Learning Together.* New York: Wiley.

Shaywitz, S. (2005) *Overcoming Dyslexia: A New and Complete Science-Based Program for Overcoming Reading Problems at Any Level.* New York: Vintage.

## Internet resources

LD OnLine at *www.ldonline.org* is a superb resource including fair, full text, useful articles. Spend an evening there! Includes ADD, writing, learning, speech, and social difficulties. In particular, see their corner for kids.

National Center for Learning Disabilities at *www.ld.org*. Mailing address: 381 Park Ave. South Suite 1401, New York, NY 10016. Phone: (001) 212-545-7510.

International Dyslexia Association at *www.interdys.org*. Mailing address: Chester Bldg, Suite 382, 8600 LaSalle Road, Baltimore, MD 21286. Phone: (001) 800-ABCD123.

*www.Schwablearning.org* has valuable brief articles covering a wide range of LD and associated problems.

## Asperger's syndrome
## Books

Attwood, T (1998) *Asperger's Syndrome: A Guide for Parents and Professionals.* London: Jessica Kingsley Publishers. An excellent (brief) diagnostic and treatment resource. See also his website at *www.tonyattwood.com.au* which includes numerous excellent articles and an Asperger's rating scale.

Bashe, P., and Kirby, B. (2001) *The OASIS Guide to Asperger Syndrome.* New York: Crown Publishers. Another excellent and complete resource (lengthy), written empathetically and fairly. See also their comprehensive OASIS website and support group which formed the basis for the book at *www.udel.edu/bkirby/asperger/*.

Jackson, L. (2002) *Freaks, Geeks, and Asperger Syndrome: A User Guide to Adolescence.* London: Jessica Kingsley Publishers. Filled with understanding and advice from a teen with Asperger's.

Willey, L.H. (1999) *Pretending to be Normal: Living with Asperger's Syndrome.* London: Jessica Kingsley Publishers. A powerful, elegant autobiography that traces the struggles faced by children and adults with Asperger's. Several appendices provide practical advice for students, employees, and parents.

## Internet resources

*Writing Social Stories with Carol Gray* (2000) is a video workshop available from *www.FutureHorizons-autism.com.*

## Non-verbal learning disabilities
## Internet resources

Dinklage, D. *Asperger's Disorder and Nonverbal Learning Disabilities: How are These Two Disorders Related to Each Other?* at *www.nldontheweb.org/dinklage_1.htm.*

Thompson, S. *Nonverbal Learning Disorders* at *www.nldontheweb.org/thompson-1.htm.*

## Semantic-pragmatic language disorder
### Internet resources

Bowen, C. *Semantic and Pragmatic Difficulties* at *http://members.tripod.com/Caroline_Bowen/spld.htm.*

See also an excellent site on SPLD at *www.geocities.com/DeniseV2/* and *www.hyperlexia.org/sp1.html* for an article by Margo Sharp.

## Sensory integration dysfunction
### Books

Kranowitz, C.S. (1998) *The Out-of-Sync Child: Recognizing and Coping with Sensory Integration Dysfunction.* New York: Skylight Press. This book covers the diagnosis and treatment of sensory integration disorders. Makes sense out of a very broad topic. New edition forthcoming.

### Internet resources

Stevens, L.C. *Sensory Integration Dysfunction in Young Children* has understandable and complete information at *www.tsbvi.edu/Outreach/seehear/fall97/sensory.htm.*

Hatch-Rasmussen, C. *Sensory Integration* at *www.autism.org/si.html.*

Lips, D. *A Day in the Life of Alex: Coping with Sensory Integration Dysfunction* at *www.comeunity.com/disability/sensory_integration/a-day.html.*

Miller-Kuhaneck, H. *Home Activities for Children with Sensory Processing Disorder* at *www.spdnetwork.org/aboutspd/homeactivities.html.*

Brick, V., and Shatako, J. *Oral Defensiveness Activities* at *www.comeunity.com/disability/sensory_integration/activities-oral.html.*

## Tourette's syndrome
### Books

Dornbush, M., and Pruitt, S. (1995) *Teaching the Tiger.* California: Hope Press. This text is an entire book of accommodations for Tourette's students. Many of these ideas apply to ADHD and LD students as well.

### Internet resources

Tourette Syndrome "Plus" at *www.tourettesyndrome.net* is an awesome and practical site on Tourette's, OCD, rage, etc. by Leslie E. Packer.

Tourette Syndrome Association lists its local chapters at *www.tsa-usa.org.*

## Bipolar depression
## Books

Papolos, D. (2002) *The Bipolar Child.* New York: Broadway Books. This is an excellent diagnostic and treatment resource. This book has brought awareness about bipolar depression in children into the public realm.

## Internet resources

*www.bpkids.org* is a great site on bipolar depression.

## Oppositional defiant disorder
## Books

Barkley, R. (1998) *Your Defiant Child.* New York: Guilford Press. A book for caregivers of oppositional/defiant children by a careful researcher and thinker.

Greene, R.W. (1999) *The Explosive Child: A New Approach for Understanding and Parenting Easily Frustrated, Chronically Inflexible Children.* London: HarperCollins. A must read for parents of inflexible-explosive children who do not respond well to typical reward systems—whether or not they have oppositional defiant disorder. This book is wonderfully and empathically written.

## Central auditory processing disorders
## Books

Bellis, T.J. (2003) *When the Brain Can't Hear.* New York: Simon & Schuster.

## Internet resources

Florida Department of Education. *Auditory Processing Disorders* at *www.firn.edu/doe/bin00014/pdf/y2001–9.pdf.*

Extracts from *From Central Auditory Processing Skills to Language and Literacy,* Speech Pathology Australia, National Conference, Adelaide, May 8–12, 2000. *http://home.iprimus.com.au/rboon/CAPD.htm.*

Bland-Stewart, L. *Children Who Present With LD and Confirmed CAP Abilities: An Outline Remediation Approach* at *www.ldonline.org/ld_indepth/process_deficit/bland_stewart.html.*

Paton, J. *Central Auditory Processing Disorders* at *www.ldonline.org/ld_indepth/process_deficit/capd_paton.html.*

# References

American Psychiatric Association (APA) (1994) *Diagnostic and Statistical Manual of Mental Disorders* (4th edition). Washington, DC: American Psychiatric Association.

Barkley, R. (1998) *Attention-Deficit Hyperactivity Disorder: A Handbook for Diagnosis and Treatment* (2nd edition). New York: The Guilford Press.

Barkley, R. (2000) *Taking Charge of ADHD*. New York: The Guilford Press.

Barkley, R.A., Fischer, M., Edelbrock, C., and Smallish, L. (1990) "The adolescent outcome of hyperactive children diagnosed by research criteria: An 8-year prospective follow-up study." *Journal of the American Academy of Child and Adolescent Psychiatry 29*, 546–557.

Bernstein, G. and Layne, A. (2004) "Separation anxiety disorder and generalized anxiety disorder." In J. Wiener and M. Dulcan (eds) *Textbook of Child and Adolescent Psychiatry* (3rd edition). Arlington, VA: American Psychiatric Publishing, pp.557–575.

Covey, S.R. (1989) *The Seven Habits of Highly Effective People: Restoring the Character Ethic*. New York: Simon & Schuster.

Feinstein, C. and Phillips, I. (2004) "Developmental disorders of learning, motor skills, and communication." In J. Wiener and M. Dulcan (eds) *Textbook of Child and Adolescent Psychiatry* (3rd edition). Arlington, VA: American Psychiatric Publishing, pp.351–378.

Freeman, J.B., Garcia, A.M., Swedo, S.E., *et al.* (2004) "Obsessive-Compulsive Disorder" in J. Wiener and M. Dulcan (eds) *Textbook of Child and Adolescent Psychiatry* (3rd edition). Arlington, VA: American Psychiatric Publishing, pp.575–588.

Florida Department of Education (2001) *Auditory Processing Disorders*. Technical Assistance Paper FY 2001-9. Available from *www.firn.edu/doe/bin00014/pdf/y2001-9.pdf*

Gray, C. and White, A.L. (eds) (2002) *My Social Stories Book*. London: Jessica Kingsley Publishers.

Greene, R.W. (1999) *The Explosive Child: A New Approach for Understanding and Parenting Easily Frustrated, Chronically Inflexible Children*. London: HarperCollins.

Jensen, P.S., Hinshaw, S.P., Swanson, J.M. *et al.* (2001) "Findings from the NIMH Multimodal Treatment Study of ADHD (MTA); implications and applications for primary care providers." *Journal of Developmental and Behavioral Pediatrics 22*, 1, 60–73.

King, R. and Leckman, J. (2004) "Tic disorders." In J. Wiener and M. Dulcan (eds) *Textbook of Child and Adolescent Psychiatry* (3rd edition). Arlington, VA: American Psychiatric Publishing, pp.709–715.

Kranowitz, C.S. (1998) *The Out-Of-Sync Child: Recognizing and Coping with Sensory Integration Dysfunction.* New York: Skylight Press.

Kupperman, P., Bligh, S. and Barouski, K. (n.d.) *Hyperlexia.* *www.hyperlexia.org/hyperlexia.html*

Olfson, M. Ganeroff, M.J. and Marcus, S.C. *et al.* "National trends in the treatment of attention deficit hyperactivity disorder." *American Journal of Psychiatry 160,* 6, 1071–7.

Osman, B.B. (1997) *Learning Disabilities and ADHD: A Family Guide to Living and Learning Together.* New York: Wiley.

Packer, L. (2005) *http://www.tourettesyndrome.net/*

Phelan, T.W. (1994) *Surviving Your Adolescents: How to Manage and Let Go of Your 13–18 Year Olds.* Glen Ellyn, IL: Child Management Press.

Ratey, J.J. and Johnson, C. (1998) *Shadow Syndromes: The Mild Forms of Mental Disorder That Sabotage Us.* New York: Bantam Books.

Schatschneider, C. and Torgesen, J.K. (2004) "Using our current understanding of dyslexia to support early identification and intervention." *Journal of Child Neurology 19,* 759–765.

Schminky, M. and Baran, J. (1999) "CAPD: an overview of assessment and management practices." *Deaf-Blind Perspectives,* Fall.

Shalev, R. (2004) "Developmental dyscalculia." *Journal of Child Neurology 19,* 10, 765–771.

Shore, K. (2002) *Special Kids Problem Solver: Ready-to-Use Interventions for Helping All Students with Academic, Behavioral, and Physical Problems.* San Francisco: Jossey-Bass.

Szymanski, L.S. and Kaplan, L.C. (2004) "Mental Retardation." In J. Weiner and M. Dulcan (eds) *Textbook of Child and Adolescent Psychiatry* (3rd edition). Arlington, VA: American Psychiatric Publishing, pp.221–261.

Thompson, S. (1996) "Non verbal learning disabilities." *http://www.nldontheweb.org/thompson-1.htm*

Torgesen, J. (2004) "Avoiding the devastating downward spiral: The evidence that early intervention prevents reading failure." *American Educator,* Fall, 6–9.

Tynan, W.D. (2003) "Oppositional defiant disorder." Article in *www.emedicine.com*

Waslick, B. and Greenhill, L. (2004) "Attention deficit/hyperactivity disorder." In J. Wiener and M. Dulcan (eds) *Textbook of Child and Adolescent Psychiatry* (3rd edition). Arlington, VA: American Psychiatric Publishing.

Wattenberg, R. (2004) "Waiting rarely works: 'Late bloomers' usually just wilt." *American Educator,* Fall, 10–11.

Weller, E., Weller, R., and Danielyan, A. (2004) "Mood disorders in prepubertal children." In J. Wiener and M. Dulcan (eds) *Textbook of Child and Adolescent Psychiatry* (3rd edition). Arlington, VA: American Psychiatric Publishing, pp.411–435.

Wiener, J.M. and Dulcan, M.K. (eds) (2004) *Textbook of Child and Adolescent Psychiatry* (3rd edition). Arlington, VA: American Psychiatric Publishing.

Wilens, T.E., Faracne, S.V., Biederman, J. *et al.* (2003) "Does stimulant therapy of attention deficit/hyperactivity disorder beget substance abuse? A meta-analytic review of the literature." *Pediatrics 111,* 11, 179–85.

Willey, L.H. (1999) *Pretending to Be Normal: Living with Asperger's Syndrome.* London: Jessica Kingsley Publishers.

Zeigler Dendy, C. (1995) *Teenagers with ADD: A Parents' Guide.* Bethesda, MD: Woodbine House.

# About the Authors

**Martin L. Kutscher, MD** is board certified in pediatrics and in neurology with special competency in child neurology. Dr. Kutscher received his B.A. from Columbia University and his M.D. from Columbia University's College of Physicians and Surgeons. He completed a pediatric internship and residency at Temple University's St. Christopher's Hospital for Children. His neurology residency and pediatric neurology fellowship were completed at the Albert Einstein College of Medicine. He is currently a member of the Departments of Pediatrics and Neurology of New York Medical College in Valhalla, New York. Dr. Kutscher is a partner of Pediatric Neurological Associates in White Plains, New York, where he has worked with special needs children for the past 17 years. He is author of *ADHD Book: Living Right Now!* (2003, Neurology Press) and of *www.PediatricNeurology.com*.

**Tony Attwood, PhD** is recognized as the world's leading authority on Asperger's syndrome. Dr. Attwood received an honours degree in psychology from the University of Hull, master's degree in clinical psychology from the University of Surrey, and Ph.D. from the University of London. He has written the groundbreaking text *Asperger's Syndrome: A Guide for Parents and Professionals* (1998, Jessica Kingsley Publishers), and has published and lectured widely around the world.

**Robert R. Wolff, MD** is board certified in pediatrics and in neurology with special competency in child neurology. Dr. Wolff received his B.A. from Princeton and his M.D. from Boston University School of Medicine. He completed a pediatric internship and residency at Yale-New Haven Hospital. His neurology residency and pediatric neurology fellowship were completed at Columbia University's Neurological Institute. He is currently a member of the Departments of Pediatrics and Neurology of New York Medical College in Valhalla, New York. Dr. Wolff has been a partner of Pediatric Neurological Associates in White Plains, New York for 25 years.

**Joelle Glick** is a premedical student at Cornell University. Her major is in biology.

# Author Index

American Psychiatric Association
41, 63, 94, 95, 127, 131,
155–6, 171, 172
Attwood, T. 118

Baran, J. 179
Barkley, R.A. 24, 27, 30, 31, 43,
44, 49, 50
Bernstein, G. 128, 130

Chandler, J. 175
Covey, S.R. 36

Danielyan, A. 160

Feinstein, C. 64, 66, 69, 78
Florida Department of Education
184
Freeman, J.B. 201

Garnett, K. 76
Gray, C. 112–3, 121
Greene, R.W. 30, 36, 49
Greenhill, L. 149

Jackson, L. 115
Jensen, P.S. 59
Johnson, C. 16

Kaplan, L.C. 82
King, R. 149
Kranowitz, C.S. 137
Kupperman, P. 101

Layne, A. 128, 130
Leckman, J. 149

Olfson, M. 51
Osman, B. 63, 64, 66–7

Packer, L. 132, 148, 152
Papolos, D. 163
Phelan, T.W. 32–3
Phillips, I. 64, 66, 69, 78

Ratey, J.J. 16

Schatschneider, C. 72
Schminky, M. 179
Shalev, R. 76
Shore, K. 73, 129, 132
Silver, L. 31
Szymanski, L.S. 82

Thompson, S. 96–7
Torgesen, J.K. 71, 72
Tynan, W.D. 172, 173

Waslick, B. 149
Wattenberg, R. 71
Weller, E. & R. 160, 163, 169
White, A. Leigh 121
Wilens, T.E. 191, 196
Willey, L.H. 25, 30, 89, 91

Zeigler Dendy, C. 33–4